Alfonso Gálvez

FLORILEGIUM

Second Edition

Translated from the Spanish by
Macia K. Maranski and Fr. Lope Pascual

New Jersey
U.S.A. – 2023

CATALOGING DATA

Author: Gálvez, Alfonso, 1932–2022
Title: Florilegium, Second Edition

| First Printing | New Jersey, 2013 |
| Second Printing | New Jersey, 2023 |

Library of Congress Control Number: 2023917314

ISBN: 978-1-953170-35-4
978-1-953170-36-1 (e-book)

**Published by
Shoreless Lake Press
P.O. Box 157
Stewartsville, New Jersey 08886**

Note to the second edition

The original text has been preserved, but the references of many of the poems have been updated and adapted to the new edition of them which the author revised in 2020, and which are published under the title "Cantos del Final del Camino".

Likewise, an index and quotations of Scripture have been added, which were not present in the first edition.

INTRODUCTION

A detailed study of the nature of Poetry would immediately stumble upon mystery. And the same is true, more specifically, with regard to religious Poetry, which also raises issues difficult to resolve.

Many will probably dismiss this suggestion by affirming that Poetry has nothing to do with mystery. And as for religious Poetry, they would be quick to say that it is merely poetic art with specifically religious content. The subject, however, is much more complex than it may seem. One cannot honestly consider certain matters settled which, although apparently simple at first glance, are extraordinarily deep the moment one begins to ponder them.

The question of Poetry is one of many issues whose elucidation everybody claims to know the very moment it is raised. But, when it comes to explaining it, nobody can do it satisfactorily.

Poetry is the expression of the Beautiful —the *Pulchrum*— through words, whether oral or written; as Painting uses pictures, or Music the sound.

But the *Pulchrum*, together with the *Bonum* and the *Verum* —the so–called *transcendentals*— are in turn the epiphany or demonstration of *Being*.[1] Hence what is often presented as Poetry, but whose content is naught because it either *suggests nothing* or has no beauty, actually has little to do with what might be regarded as a product of the Muses of Poetry. But we are not going to dwell here on a subject that has been dealt with by this author in some detail elsewhere in his works.[2]

As for religious Poetry, it could be defined as poesy whose content is circumscribed to the beliefs of Religion. Unfortunately, taking into account the conditions set forth herein as necessary to qualify a literary work as authentic Poetry, it soon becomes clear that [real] religious poetry is surprisingly scarce.

---

[1] To which the *Unum* must be added.

[2] *Commentaries on the Song of Songs*, Vol. I, Shoreless Lake Press, New Jersey, 1995, pp. 195–228. *Commentaries to the Song of Songs*, Vol. II, Shoreless Lake Press, New Jersey, 2006, pp. 353–375. *Cantos del Final del Camino*, Segunda Edición, Shoreless Lake Press, New Jersey, 2020, pp. V–XL. Editor's note: A new printing of the *Commentaries on the Song of Songs* was made in 2022.

First of all, because two realities as dissimilar as *verse* and *poetry* should not be confused. Of course, the latter can be set in either verse or prose... provided that beauty is contained in either construction. Likewise, it must be borne in mind that a literary work cannot be considered poetic merely because it is written in verse; it is also essential that its content shine with beauty, *expressed in this case through words*. Hence, in terms of religious themes, a merely *pious verse*, regardless of how fervent it may be, does not yet meet —based on that fact alone— the conditions required by the true poetic art.

Among the few examples of what can be considered as true religious poetry, the mystical poetry of Saint John of the Cross stands out as an isolated effort whose undoubted quality is beyond question. There are other religious poems, not very numerous, also worthy of study: for example, some mystical rhymes of Saint Teresa of Avila; the famous anonymous Sonnet to the Crucified Christ, *I am not moved, my Lord, to love You*; certain *Odes* by Fray Luis de Leon; or particular sonnets by Baltasar de Alcázar.

Perhaps the reader will miss in this list some other classical poets of the Spanish Language. The reason for their absence is that they have hardly cultivated religious Poetry. And as for the few compositions that Lope de Vega, for example, dedicated to religious poetry, nothing is to be said except that they do not seem to be his best work. Other than that, we can also refer to some of the *Odes* by Fray Luis de Leon as works also noteworthy in this field. Otherwise, little can be said of most modern poets in regard to religious Poetry —much less when one takes into consideration the necessary requisites mentioned above to grant poetic value to a literary composition. In the case of contemporary poets, all we can do is make a comprehensive reference to the multitude of current religious *poets*, whose ambition and good faith are almost as considerable as their lack of poetic inspiration.

The reader should not be surprised that we make no reference to foreign poets, except for some very rare exceptions. The reason for this is that Poetry *is untranslatable to any language other than the one in which it has been written.* Indeed, ideas or concepts can be expressed, through prose, in many and varied ways that ultimately do not depend exclusively on specific words (hence synonyms and the multitude of literary styles) and, therefore, on a particular language. In Poetry, on the contrary, its content depends *on both the concepts and the words expressly used in a given case.* And since the latter are quite different when translated into another language, they lose the beauty of expression when words are changed (the concept may be the same, but the word that expresses it is not). Not to mention the demands imposed by rhyme, and the otherwise indisputable fact that words expressing the same concept can be beautiful in one language (within or outside the same context) but not in another.

On the other hand, true poetic art, expressive in this case of lofty religious or mystical feelings through the beauty of language, does not need to use pious or religious words; which is clearly demonstrated, for example, in the poetry of Saint John of the Cross.

Moreover, one should not rush to equate religious poetry with mystical poetry. For if it is true that all mystic poetry is religious, not all religious poetry is mystical. And if in the field of Christian Spirituality there is a difference, even an essential difference, between simple prayer and contemplative prayer, then this distinction must be taken into consideration, *mutatis mutandis*, in regard to these two types of religious poetry. (Not forgetting what was said above about piety not being synonymous with beauty.)

Sometimes we tend to believe that the element of beauty is never absent from religious poetry, by virtue of its being religious and since beauty is a necessary ingredient of the poetic nature. The truth, however, is that *beauty* is not necessarily connected with the *religious* element, by first intention at least. In the Bible, there are very expressive passages which support the opposite: *I am a worm and no man; a reproach of men, and the outcast of the people*;[3] not to allude to many of the Prophets and even to the New Testament. For the purpose of the Bible is not artistic but didactic, notwithstanding the fact that it contains eminently poetic books, such as *The Song of Songs*.

Someone might argue, not without certain justification, that the sublime glory of the tragedy of the Cross, together with the goodness of God Who has given Christians the possibility of sharing in the sufferings and death of His Son, possess the ineffable beauty that might be expected of one of the greatest divine plans. However, it should also be noted that the magnificence that emerges from such graces so generously granted to man is perceptible in the mind of the disciple of Jesus Christ *in an indirect way* only; both as to the content of this magnificence and its perceived effect and as regards the scope of pure reflection... which has little to do with Aesthetics, whose essential character is to show an object merely as *Pulchrum* directly and primarily to the perception of human beings. It is not reflection but Aesthetics that refers to the direct

---

[3]Ps 21:7.

contemplation of the *Pulchrum*. Saint Thomas already said that it is through the senses of sight and hearing that man is able to perceive beauty.

This book is a simple commentary in the form of short chapters on some of the author's poetic compositions that have been compiled in the booklet *Cantos del Final del Camino*;[4] they do not try to delve too deeply into topics already very difficult, in order that it may be accessible to a large majority of people.

Since the main purpose of Poetry is none other than to express feelings that are otherwise inexpressible, by trying to get to the depths of the soul or to that place where simple prose cannot reach, it seems that any commentary to a poetic work will certainly present difficulties. Usually, the content or meaning of a poetic work explained in plain prose satisfies almost no one. As is apparent, for example, in the prose explanations of Saint John of the Cross; the contrast between the luminous *beauty* of his poetry and the *roughness* and complexity of his prose is quite notorious; and the parallelism that the Saint seeks to establish between the lyricism of his brilliant stanzas, on the one

---

[4]*Cantos del Final del Camino*, Segunda Edición. Shoreless Lake Press, New Jersey, 2020 (henceforth *CFC*).

hand, and the corresponding doctrinal conclusions, on the other, is not always evident.

And yet, if Poetry is able to reach the corners of the soul where plain prose cannot reach, *not even Poetry can say everything.* It is true that the human heart has been endowed with the capacity to love, with the power to touch the infinite; therefore, it can never be satiated —*until our heart rests in Thee*, as Saint Augustine said. Hence simple prose is always able to add something to Poetry; at least as a plow for her new fields that, in turn, can be sown and grown.

And since Poetry, if true, is always the expression of Love that is incapable of understanding limits and measurements, which impel that

> *Many waters cannot quench love,*
> *Neither can floods drown it...*[5]

In the same identical way it could be said that

> *Neither oceans of words can ever exhaust it,*
> *Nor elaborate speeches explain it.*

---

[5]Sg 8:7.

Hence, if Poetry can supply, if only partially and through the beauty of its lyricism, that which plain language is unable to express, then it is conceivable that perhaps prose can always add something to poetry. For it is clear that one finiteness can be supplemented by another; and both, in turn, by new ones... until all of them arrive finally at the only Infinity that alone can fill the heart of man and comprehend everything.

I

As you walk towards hills above,
Allow me to walk with you, pilgrim, my friend,
And see if he whom I love
Gives us his wine to drink of,
In reaching together our long journey's end.[1]

Christian life is like the existence of someone exiled in a foreign land; his life is an endless odyssey toward his own Country: *We have not here a lasting city, but we seek one that is to come.*[2]

That was how the great masters of Christian spirituality understood the unfolding of the existence of a disciple

---

[1] *CFC*, n. 1. In the Spanish original: *Si vas hacia el otero,/ deja que te acompañe, peregrino,/ a ver si el que yo quiero/ nos da a beber su vino/ en acabando juntos el camino.*

[2] Heb 13:14.

of Jesus Christ: *The Ascent of Mount Carmel*, of Saint John of the Cross; *The Soul's Journey into God*, of Saint Bonaventure; the wearying walk through the various *Mansions* to reach the depths of the *Interior Castle*, of Saint Teresa of Avila. Even Jesus Christ described this existential journey of His followers as a voyage made along a difficult, narrow, and steep path: *How narrow is the gate, and strait is the way that leads to Life, and few there are who find it!*[3]

Therefore, the first thing patent to a Christian is that his life is being spent in a foreign land, *away from his Homeland* toward which he undoubtedly is walking. This fact has a double aspect: one negative and one positive.

Negative for those who are determined to make the land they currently inhabit their definitive Homeland. Today, this is the most widespread attitude, even within the Church Herself among the circles of modern progressive theology —to the point that high–ranking members of Her Hierarchy share it. This approach leads to a heartbreaking failure that can hardly ever be reversed.

There are also countless numbers of people, however, who seem to think that there is no way along which one can

---

[3] Mt 7:14.

walk; as is expressed, for example, by these well–known verses of Antonio Machado:

> *Wayfarer, there is no way,*
> *Way is made as we walk.*[4]

The lack of a road that may guide man's steps to the real Homeland, where his final Destiny awaits him, is a typical tenet of pagan ideologies. For Atheism, man is a being who wanders aimlessly until he ends up in nothingness, according to an idea of human life as something empty of content and devoid of meaning. In the words of Jesus Christ Himself, he who does not follow Him *walketh in darkness.*[5] Thus the Christian is well aware that he is an itinerant and tireless searcher:

> *My loves to search for there,*
> *Amongst these mountains and ravines I'll stray,*
> *Nor pluck flowers, nor for fear*
> *Of prowling beast delay,*
> *But pass through forts and frontiers on my way.*[6]

---

[4]Most likely the poet, rather than denying the wandering condition of human life, was echoing the difficulty of a path that every human being must be building for himself; a path which is filled with eventful episodes.

[5]Jn 8:12.

[6]Saint John of the Cross. *Spiritual Canticle.*

> *At early dawn still rosy*
> *I searched the thickets of the woods with great pace,*
> *For Him Who enamours me*
> *With the splendor of His face;*
> *As he compels me to meet Him at great haste.*[7]

The positive aspect of this itinerancy is provided by those who know that they are walking through an uncharted and inhospitable land; with the hopeful certainty that a Homeland is waiting for them after a rough and difficult voyage as their final Home. This approach is exclusive to the disciples of Jesus Christ, who know well, because the Master Himself has said it, that this way exists and has been drawn with a firm hand: *Whither I go you know the way... I am the Way, and the Truth, and the Life.*[8]

Indeed, the path of Christian existence is fraught with difficulties and setbacks (the narrow and difficult road); the main one being that the disciple of Jesus Christ is forced to live in the *Dark Night* of the soul, brought about in him by the absence of his Lord; hence the life of the

---

[7] *CFC.* n. 89. In the Spanish original: *En la rosada aurora/ salí a buscar, del bosque en la espesura,/ a Aquél que me enamora,/ que me azara en rubor por su hermosura/ y que corra a su encuentro me apresura.*

[8] Jn 14: 4.6.

disciple is filled with longings and fed with hope because of His absence which he on his own can never fully comprehend:

> *At night he left for the distant mountain range,*
> *At night he followed the road around the bend,*
> *At night I was left in foreign lands and strange,*
> *At night I was left alone without my friend.*[9]

However, the disciple has a clear consciousness that he is walking toward his Homeland as he sees himself climbing to the summit of Mount Carmel or to the very crest of the hill, as the poems says. And this is enough to fill his heart with a sure hope that will never let him down, according to the Apostle's words: *Tribulation worketh patience; and patience, tested virtue; and tested virtue, hope. And hope does not let us down.*[10] Thus, all the sufferings and setbacks which life provides him *have a meaning for him* which takes him away from the bitterness and despair that overtake those who live without Jesus Christ; that is, those who live without any hope and without any knowledge of the reason for their existence.

---

[9] *CFC*, n. 23. In the Spanish original: *De noche se marchó hacia la montaña,/ De noche se perdió por le sendero,/ De noche me dejó, por tierra extraña,/ De noche me quedé sin compañero.*

[10] Rom 5: 3–5.

In some way, walking in the direction of Mount Carmel, while *still* a journey, is also somehow being in the Homeland, which is *already possessed for the time being*, if only in the form of a pledge or first fruits: *You have come to Mount Zion and to the city of the living God, the heavenly Jerusalem where the millions of angels have gathered for the festival, and to the Church of the firstborn who are written in the heavens.*[11]

The Christian does not make his way alone —hence the yearning expression *let me accompany you, pilgrim—*; he walks in the company of his Master. Consequently he has enough reasons for crossing the Valley of Tears while listening to Him and enjoying His company; which provides for him now a feeling of exultation that is but the first fruits of what one day will be Perfect Joy for him: *The friend of the Bridegroom, who stands and hears him, rejoices greatly at the Bridegroom's voice. This my joy therefore is fulfilled.*[12]

This joy is even more complete when the Christian realizes that he is journeying accompanied by his brethren. As we will see, love for God passes, as a condition, through love for one's brothers; although God is, in the last analysis, the fountain and beginning of all love.

---

[11]Heb 12: 22–23.

[12]Jn 3:29.

II

Allow me to walk with you, pilgrim, my friend...

The Christian never walks alone on his pilgrimage towards his Homeland, he is accompanied by his brothers. Created by Love and to love, his final Destiny is Uncreated Love... Who cannot be reached by man, once he has set out, unless he has previously lived created love (1 Jn 4:20).

The Christian loves his brethren because he and they are children of God (1 Jn 3:1). We must take into account that as supernatural love between father and son is immensely superior to the natural love between them according to the flesh, the same can be said about fraternal love; even more so, since both brothers belong to the same Mystical Body of Christ and have been redeemed by the same Blood.

Nevertheless, the foremost reason to love our brothers in the faith is based on a simple and deep one: he who truly loves Jesus Christ *also loves everything that is loved by Him.* How can a man not love all things that the beloved person makes the object of his love? Hence Saint John clearly says that *He that loveth not his brother whom he hath seen cannot love God whom he hath not seen.*[1]

But if we have established that love is the source of all joy (in Galatians 5:22, charity is the first of the fruits which the Holy Spirit causes in the soul; joy is the second), one soon realizes that love for our brethren, far from being merely an obligation imposed upon us by a precept, is a constant source of perfect joy worthy of such a name and able to make the soul exultant. Even the Old Testament proclaimed this with picturesque words:

> *Behold, how good and how pleasant*
> *It is for brethren to dwell together in unity!*
> *It is like the precious ointment upon the head,*
> *That ran down upon the beard,*
> *The beard of Aaron.*[2]

---

[1] 1 Jn 4:20.
[2] Ps 132: 1–2.

Elsewhere the benefits derived from the unity of brothers is expounded: *A brother helped by a brother is like a fortified city, like an unassailable wall.*[3]

But it is the New Testament that truly authenticates fraternal love; it was Jesus Christ who promulgated it as His *new commandment* and the hallmark by which His disciples should be recognized (Jn 13: 34–35).

The pilgrimage to the future city (Heb 13:14) passes through a narrow, steep, and difficult road (Mt 7:14). And God, in His endless kindness, wanted man to travel it accompanied by others; giving him the opportunity to practice that love which one day, when he has reached the goal, would become a vast and mighty river in Heaven. There the part would be turned into the whole; and the rehearsal would submit before the formal opening and definitive presentation of the play.

In this way, the distressing walk through the Valley of Tears has been transformed, thanks to the love and goodness of God, into the joy subsequent to that happy feeling of being accompanied by someone one loves. As Saint John the Baptist understood quite well: *He that hath the bride is the bridegroom; and yet the friend of*

---

[3]Prov 18:19, according to the Vulgate and the Greek text of the Septuagint.

the bridegroom, who standeth and heareth him, is filled with joy because of the bridegroom's voice: this my joy therefore is fulfilled.[4] Walking hand in hand with love gives wings to the journey and makes the weight of even the most ponderous yoke become easy and its burden light (Mt 11:30):

> *Come with me, come walk with me,*
> *Together we shall cross the ford and mountain,*
> *And together search to see*
> *The footprints of the Loved One,*
> *And together reach his side when day is done.*[5]

Unfortunately, the heart of man has become so diminished because of sin that he has forgotten all this. Man, having come to think of these realities as something too broad and lofty (the sublime cannot abide within the vulgar), has replaced them with blunt, ordinary concepts, more adaptable to the coarseness of man's feelings and also more comprehensible to those who have chosen to debase their own condition. This is how charity —true

---

[4] Jn 3:29.

[5] *CFC*, n. 12. In the Spanish original: *Acude y caminemos, / y juntos cruzaremos por el vado, / y juntos buscaremos / las huellas del Amado, / y juntos llegaremos a su lado.*

love— has been replaced by *solidarity*; love conversation has become just *dialogue* (understood in a merely human way, whose main feature is to never accomplish anything); finally, veneration of our brothers out of love has given way to respect for *human rights*. And all of this goes on in a world of hypocrisy in which there is neither solidarity nor true dialogue, and where human rights are nothing more than a pipe dream or false illusion that no one can find anywhere.

It is a sad misfortune that those who, once destined to walk together in the joy of brotherly love, have totally forgotten that they could have softened the road, always rough and steep, with the sweet joy of traversing it in the dear company of those whom they loved..., while also feeling themselves loved in return:

> *And then together we'll climb*
> *To the hill where rue and cumin are pungent;*
> *And arriving in due time,*
> *The road now traveled and spent,*
> *We'll drink your sweet wine with joy and merriment.*[6]

---

[6] *CFC.* n. 15. In the Spanish original: *Amado, subiremos/ al monte de la ruda y del comino,/ y luego que lleguemos/ al cabo del camino,/ alegres beberemos de tu vino.*

III

And see if he whom I love
Gives us his wine to drink of...

At the institution of the Eucharist on the night of the Last Supper, Jesus Christ told His disciples: *I say to you, I will not drink from henceforth of the fruit of the vine until that day when I shall drink it new with you in the Kingdom of my Father.*[1]

The time to drink the fruit of the vine along with the Master, once we are in the Father's House, will be at the End of a Road which, until that moment, had been a long and painful journey. As the Apostle said: *I have fought a*

---

[1] Mt 26:29.

good fight, I have finished my race.[2] It will be the moment
for which the disciple had been yearning for such a long
time and for which he had been created:

> *My Love, I will climb with you*
> *Hills where rue and cumin and rosemary grows,*
> *And when our travels are through,*
> *And journey comes to a close,*
> *We will drink your wine with joy in sweet repose.*[3]

The image of wine has a particular relevance in Holy
Scripture. It is always associated with the idea of marriage
(remember the account of the Wedding at Cana) as well
as with the love between the Bridegroom and the bride
which has reached its plenitude. It is a metaphor, after all.
But given that in the mind of man this liquor is always
associated with the idea of joy —*Wine makes glad the
heart of man,* says the psalmist[4]—, and given also that
joy is the fruit of love, both caused by the Holy Spirit in
the soul, there is nothing unusual about the comparison

---

[2] 2 Tim 4:7.

[3] *CFC,* n. 15. In the Spanish original: *Amado, subiremos/ al monte
de la ruda y del comino,/ y luego que lleguemos/ al cabo del camino,/
alegres beberemos de tu vino.*

[4] Ps 104:15.

that the bride of the *Song of Songs* makes of the loves of
the Bridegroom to the sweetness of wine:

> *Let him kiss me with the kisses of his mouth,*
> *For thy loves are sweeter than wine.*[5]

The indigence —rather, poverty and misery— of human language to formulate lofty and most sublime concepts is never more patent than when it deals with love.
And if those concepts fail to express the deep content to
which they relate, what can be said about the terms with
which the concepts are formulated...? This is why man
feels himself *doomed* to being unable to totally communicate to others, or even to understand by himself, the
unfathomable depths and ineffable greatness of the feelings that *captivate* his soul. Because of this, man's life is
spent animated by hope, punctuated by sighs, and fed by
desires; trudging along with a forward impulse in search
of the *unspeakable* that he senses, to the point of dying
with yearnings when it appears that he does not possess
it yet:

---

[5]Sg 1:2; cf. 1:4.

> *His loving eyes looked at me*
> *Before the morning sun appeared in the sky,*
> *And they wounded me gravely*
> *With such sweet love that if I*
> *Could not see them again, I would surely die.*[6]

That is why the Bridegroom of the *Song of Songs* answers the bride using the same kind of language. What else can He do if He wants to be heard and understood by her...? Hence the wonderful condescendence of Love; He *lowers* Himself to be able to establish an intimate relationship with His creature. For this reason, it will never be possible, not even in our Homeland, to understand the infinite degree of love that the Incarnation of the Son of God is:

> *How fair is thy love, my sister, my spouse!*
> *How much sweeter is thy love than wine!*
> *How fragrant your perfumes,*
> *More fragrant than all spices!*[7]

It is no wonder that poets and lovers of the world have dedicated the inspiration of their muses as well as the art

---

[6] *CFC*, n. 33. In the Spanish original: *Sus ojos me miraron/ antes que el claro sol apareciera,/ y herido me dejaron/ de amor, en tal manera,/ que sin verlos de nuevo pereciera..*

[7] Sg 4:10.

of their lyres to singing to purely human love. When it is impossible to reach what is most high and inaccessible, there is nothing but to be satisfied with what is closest. How to sing to divine love, and even to divine–human love...? Only mystics dared to do so, using all the tropes and figures of speech, always insufficient and wholly incapable of expressing the contents of a heart in love with God. Hence mystical poetry, despite its insufficiency, is what most deeply moves the human heart, wounding it until it hurts, and making it feel *that* which could have been... and was lost because of sin.

And Scripture persists in using the image of wine to speak of the *drunkenness* caused by love. For not even God Himself, in His ardent desire to communicate with men, could find better words to express the feelings of *ecstasy* —is there some other word which may say it better?— and unspeakable joy that true love produces:

> *I am come into my garden, my sister, my spouse;*
> *I have gathered my myrrh with my spice;*
> *I have eaten my honeycomb with my honey;*
> *I have drunk my wine with my milk.*[8]

But we still live in this world, and there are too many men who do not want to understand these things; hence

---

[8]Sg 5:1.

the perennial character of the words of the Gospel of Saint John: *In him was life; and the life was the light of men. And the light shineth in darkness; and the darkness did not receive it.*[9]

---

[9] Jn 1: 4–5.

IV

...In reaching together our long journey's end.

After the course of one's human life, whose duration is indeterminate and whose final hour unpredictable, it is time to delight in the rest and joy of Home: *I have fought a good fight, I have finished the race, I have kept the faith.*[1] Thus some people speak, and rightly so, of the *beauty of Christian Death*, echoing sentiments also shared by the Psalmist: *Precious in the eyes of the Lord is the death of his saints.*[2]

In fact, if it was always good to leave behind the adventures of a lifetime —at least through the *oblivion* of which the poetry of Saint John of the Cross speaks— in

---

[1] 2 Tim 4:7.
[2] Ps 116:15.

which hardships more than joys abounded; today, given the situation of our world, there are more reasons than ever to justify the joy brought about by our arrival Home. And the disciple of Jesus Christ in particular cannot but necessarily feel strange and foreign in a world that he cannot understand and which, he knows quite well, despises him. Thus the *Letter to the Hebrews*, referring to our ancient fathers in the faith, states that *All these died in faith, before receiving any of the things that had been promised, but they saw them in the far distance and welcomed them, recognizing that they were only strangers and nomads on earth... But in fact they were longing for a better homeland, their heavenly homeland. That is why God is not ashamed to be called their God, since he has founded the city for them.*[3]

Hence this beautiful farewell to his earthly existence which Saint John of the Cross described with these verses of his ineffable poetry:

> *Lost to myself I stayed*
> *My face upon my lover having laid*
> *From all endeavor ceasing:*
> *All my cares releasing*
> *Threw them amongst the lilies there to fade.*[4]

---

[3]Heb 11: 13.16.

[4]Saint John of the Cross, *Dark Night of the Soul*.

Only Saints can come out with such a genial expression calling the tribulations of this life merely *cares* that can now be left behind and simply *forgotten*. Saint John of the Cross, far from lamenting his suffered hardships, rejoices in saying that he loved them; they once were useful in helping him participate in the Existence of Jesus Christ and, more especially, in His Death; now they are precious pearls adorning his crown. And if so, how could he complain about how they affected his life? Hence the loving phrase that he lavishes upon them saying that he leaves them *amongst the lilies*.

True, as the *Book of Job* says, man's life on earth, especially a Christian's life, is warfare (Job 7:1), or a good fight, according to the well–known expression of Saint Paul (2 Tim 4:7); but one also must admit, as the *Song of Songs* says, that it is a veritable combat of love (Sg 2:4).

This completely changes the perspective of the Christian's journey through his earthly life; for human life can be equated to a joust or a tournament (1 Cor 9:25), whereas before it was considered merely as a trudge through a Valley of Tears. Now that journey is seen, however, as a contest between rivals trying to obtain victory, which does not lessen the ensuing thrill that makes the hearts of the contending parties beat in great haste. Moreover, what could come to pass when the rival against whom one is

competing happens to be God, and both antagonists have
the same chance of victory? So much so that each one may
feel compelled to run more quickly than his opponent and
arrive first at the finish:

> *If then together we follow the pathway,*
> *Let me come forward and arrive first, I pray*
> *And there at the end of the road we will find,*
> *Our toils and hard labors are left far behind.*[5]

It is indeed a virtue of love to make logic and normalcy
change the meaning, even the substance, of the things
which men would normally consider folly and absurd. Jesus Christ did not show surprise because of the Apostle
Peter's petition to walk on the waters to meet Him. On
the other hand, the servant in the Parable of the Talents
gave back to his lord *two times the amount received to
negotiate* (Mt 25:20); thus it is forever made clear that
one can give *more than what he has received*; and that if
it is true that *everything is grace and depends on grace*,
it is no less true that man has been granted the faculty
to *love in truth and with truth.* Therefore, the aphorism

---

[5]*CFC.*, n. 2. In the Spanish original: *Y aunque seguimos juntos el
sendero/ deja que me adelante yo el primero/ allí donde se acaba la
vereda/ y el duro trajinar atrás se queda.*

It is more blessed to give than to receive[6] is made real in his life. Consequently, since love is essentially *self-giving and surrender more than receiving*, it could not happen differently once one has entered the world of realities from which utopias are banished.

And given that the principles of Modernism, the *New Religion*, totally ignore what true Love and His exigencies are, it lives on fantasies which have no footing in the world of being. Because *He who loveth not knoweth not God; for God is love*,[7] the *New Religion* lives on reveries which cannot go beyond what human imagination reaches; and, as a result, it does not believe in Love. Love is something too grand and escapes this *New Religion* since it cannot overcome the limitations of the human mind and heart. Which also explains why famous and prominent modernist theologians, whose names are known to everybody, do not believe in the existence of Hell. How could they admit the possibility of *total rejection* of *total Love offered* if they do not believe in that Love?

The journey of the Christian through the Valley of Tears, as it always happens with the ways of a love which is in its pilgrimage stage, is a true *adventure* which lacks

---

[6] Acts 20:35.

[7] 1 Jn 4:8.

nothing; therefore, there are in this voyage difficult and dark moments when God seems to have vanished, as if it were impossible to find Him again.

> *To the distant stars I climbed*
> *For small vestige of your footprints to find.*
> *Hoping some to sight,*
> *While walking toward the Sun, from the Moon at night.*[8]

Until the moment arrives when, once the Road has been left behind and the entrusted task has been accomplished, it is time for the joyful and definitive union with the Beloved. It is time to make real that longed–for and awaited instant: the arrival at the shores where one enjoys forever the immense Ocean of Divine Love.

> *And so my ended woes and sorrows left me*
> *There where our lives are joined as one, by the sea*
> *Rocked with gentle waves created easily*
> *By the stirred blue waters lapping lazily.*[9]

---

[8] *CFC*, n. 7. In the Spanish original: *Subí hasta las estrellas/ en busca de vestigios de tus huellas,/ por si encontraba alguna/ caminando hacia el Sol, desde la Luna.*

[9] *CFC*, n. 105. In the Spanish original: *Y allí mis penas fueron fenecidas/ junto al mar que vio unidas nuestras vidas,/ mecido en suaves ondas, producidas/ por las azules aguas removidas.*

V

Beloved, I am longing
To taste your supper in the fresh garden air;
For once again it is spring
And mountain breezes are fair
With the rosemary, thyme, and mint that grow there.[1]

A certain man made a great supper...[2]

Supper is a daily occurrence in human life, one among many. Holy Scripture sometimes uses it as an expression

---

[1] *CFC*, n. 47. In the Spanish original: *Amado, yo quisiera/ al aire del jardín gustar tu cena,/ pues es la primavera/ y el monte ya se llena/ de romero, tomillo y hierbabuena.*

[2] Lk 14:16.

of the loving request which God addresses to man: *Behold, I am standing at the door, knocking. If any man hear my voice, and open the door, I will come in to him, and will sup with him, and he with me.*[3]

In connection with this there are key events in the life of Jesus Christ, quite meaningful and essential to men of all time, which occurred on the night of the *Last Supper*: the Institution of the Eucharist, the celebration of the First Mass in the History of Mankind, the Institution of the Priesthood, the Promulgation of the New Commandment, Christ's Message and Words of Farewell... Momentous and lofty events that go far beyond any proceedings of ordinary dinners and defy any attempt at explanation.

The book of the *Apocalypse*, in turn, uses the metaphor of *supper* to illustrate what God has prepared for those who love Him: *Blessed are they who are called unto the marriage supper of the Lamb.*[4] And then: *Come and gather yourselves together unto the great supper of God.*[5]

Saint John of the Cross, in one of his most beautiful stanzas, also refers to the inebriating nature of a distinctive and undoubtedly mystical supper:

---

[3] Rev 3:20.

[4] Rev 19:9.

[5] Rev 19:17.

> *Before the dawn comes round*
> *Here is the night, dead–hushed with all its glamours,*
> *The music without sound,*
> *The solitude that clamours*
> *The supper that revives us and enamours.*[6]

It is well known that the language of love, and even more so when it is divine–human love, often uses metaphors to express itself in some way, for it cannot resort to anything better. This is easy to understand. Nevertheless, one could ask: Why use the metaphor of *supper* to express the deepest and most intimate moments of love?

Undoubtedly *supper* time —which usually is associated with images suggested by the *night*— has constantly evoked in man the desire for rest, dialogue, and interaction with loved ones once the tiresome chores of the day have been accomplished. This moment even seems to be preferred by those in love as being the best time to enjoy the intimacy that love always desires and seeks. After all, as is shown in the history of Christian spirituality, those greatly in love with Jesus Christ always considered *contemplative* life to be superior to *active* life. For, indeed, the dialogue of love finds its proper place, along with silence,

---

[6]Saint John of the Cross, *Spiritual Canticle.*

in the tranquility provided by solitude and separation from things.

Why did Jesus choose the time of Supper to live some of the most intense moments of His existence: when He consummated His mission and summarized the most endearing content of His teachings? The question in itself does not seem to have transcendental importance, but it undoubtedly possesses some deep mystical meaning. After all, *supper* time evokes the connotation of the *end of the day*; when the labors of the day have stopped and it is the right time for resting and for sharing intimate familiar or loving moments.[7] All this before the night (in this case darkness) enfolds the world. That is why Jesus Christ said: *We must carry out the works of him who sent me, while it is day; the night cometh, when no man can work.*[8]

In this sense, the *end of the day* means, especially for the Christian, the *journey's end*, that is, the arrival at our Homeland, when the fatigue and inclemency of the road are left behind. Saint John of the Cross spoke in this

---

[7]Let us notice that Saint Augustine associates the idea of love with that of rest: *You have made us for Thyself, O Lord, and our hearts are restless until they rest in Thee.* For him Love requires rest; and rest cannot exist without love.

[8]Jn 9:4.

regard of the cares which had absorbed him during his lifetime and which he now has finally left behind, *forgotten among the lilies.* This thought is common in mystical poetry:

> *If then together we follow the pathway,*
> *Let me come forward and arrive first, I pray.*
> *And there at the end of the road we will find,*
> *Our toils and hard labors are left far behind.*[9]

The bride in the *Song of Song* seems to be equally longing to find the most propitious moments, in which silence dominates and solitude is enjoyed, to be next to the Bridegroom:

> *Come, my beloved, let us go forth into the fields;*
> *Let us lodge in the villages.*[10]

She also wants to hasten those moments; perhaps because she desires to relish them before the total darkness of night descends upon the world:

---

[9] *CFC.* n. 2. In the Spanish original: *Y aunque seguimos juntos el sendero/ deja que me adelante yo el primero/ allí donde se acaba la vereda/ y el duro trajinar atrás se queda..*

[10] Sg 7:11.

Before the day–breeze rises,
And the shadows flee, return!
Be, my love, like a gazelle,
Like a young stag, on the mountains of Bether.[11]

Evidently, there is a lesson here —among many— which may be drawn from this beautiful and poetic world of metaphors and allegories: the need that every Christian has to make good use of the *short instant* in which God offers him His Love and accept It. Life is too brief and vanishes quickly, for it is destined to reach its always unforeseeable end —*For the Son of man cometh at an hour when ye think not.*[12] Hence, two important lessons must be taken into consideration here:

First, the best part is the one very wisely chosen by Mary: *Martha, Martha, thou art careful and troubled about many things. But one thing is needful, and Mary hath chosen that good part, which shall not be taken away from her.*[13] Secondly, and in complete agreement with the first, we must ponder the exemplary advice of Saint Paul to

---

[11]Sg 2:17.
[12]Lk 12:40.
[13]Lk 10: 41–42.

the Colossians, also addressed to all Christians: *Set your affections on things above, not on things on the earth.*[14]

---

[14]Col 3: 1–2.

VI

Love for Justice.

The true disciple of Jesus Christ, given his earthly condition as a pilgrim, cannot but feel disgust at the world in which he lives.

Immersed in an environment which is increasingly pagan and inimical to God, he is forced to live in a decaying society in which the most aberrant activities have become acceptable and man has descended to levels of degradation immensely inferior even to animal behavior.

In such an environment, those who dare to oppose the world's standards are ruthlessly persecuted. Values configured over centuries of Christian civilization are now the target of the most abject contempt.

This has allowed the Kingdom of Deception to be permanently established —and supported, in turn, by new systems of manipulation of the minds which have made man happily and voluntarily embrace opting for the Lie.

Even the Church has descended into the dark abyss of a deep crisis in which her Hierarchy has not been able to impede millions of her children from falling into confusion. It is true that the Institution of the Church cannot perish, according to the promise of her Divine Founder; but it is no less true that the faithful of good will *are now being forced to look for her everywhere, for it is not always easy to find where the true Church is.*

If this is the situation, it is understandable that Christians who truly search for Jesus Christ feel a nostalgia for Heaven and are burning with ardent and vehement desires of getting away from the noise and the things of this world to be with their Lord. Thus the bride of the *Song of Songs* said:

> *Come, my beloved, let us go forth into the fields;*
> *Let us lodge in the villages.*
> *Let us go up early to the vineyards;*
> *Let us see if the vines flourish,*
> *Whether the blossoms are opening,*
> *If the pomegranate trees are in flower,*
> *There I will give thee my loves.*[1]

---

[1] Sg 7: 11–12.

Popular mystical poetry also provides a distant echo of this reality:

Let's go to grassy meadows
And await Dawn's rosy brightness in her stride,
Forgotten by friends and foes;
There in sweet peace we'll abide
And hear the morning sounds of the countryside.[2]

Taking this into account, must we then believe that Christians no longer consider themselves citizens of the earthly city? Are they perchance to be regarded as deserters or as being somehow indifferent to the things of this world?

The question could be countered by simply denying the assumption. It is commonsensical that Christians are equally concerned with both spheres, heaven and earth; and it is not likely that the idea of ceasing to work on building the earthly city, as full citizens they are, has ever crossed the mind of any of them. This response, though true, would still be somewhat simplistic. The problem is far more complicated than it seems; for it is necessary to

---

[2] *CFC.* n. 106. In the Spanish original: *Vayamos a los prados/ y a la rosada aurora esperaremos,/ de todos olvidados./ Y allí nos quedaremos/ y el despertar del campo escucharemos.*

recognize that the disciple of Jesus Christ is destined to live under a tension which is paradoxical and not adapted to simple solutions.

Jesus Christ was careful to emphasize that His disciples, although they did not belong to this world, should remain in it; He raised His petition to the Father *to not take them out of this world, but to deliver them from the Evil One* (Jn 17:15). Moreover, as the Parable of the Talents points out, the coins are given to the servants *not so they could keep them, but so that they could negotiate with them until their Lord comes back and takes a reckoning; and so the lazy servant is cast into outer darkness* (Mt 25: 14 ff). Saint Paul, in turn, believes that he will finally receive the crown of justice *after having fought a good fight and finished the race* (2 Tim 4:7). In fact, the whole of Revelation always insists that each will receive compensation *according to his works.*[3]

However, it will always be true for the disciple of Jesus Christ that his heart, like the heart of Mary who was able to choose the better part (Lk 10:42), will always tend to escape from this world to be with his Lord. And so, for example, Saint Paul said: *I am hard-pressed by these two:*

---

[3]In addition to the passages in the Gospels, see, for example, Rom 2:6; Rev 2:23; 18:6; 20: 12–13.

the desire I have to depart, and to be with Christ; which is far better. Nevertheless to abide in the flesh is more needful for you.[4] Thus his advice to the Colossians: *Seek those things which are above... Set your affection on things above, not on things on the earth.*[5]

Hence Christians need to recognize the *tense,* heartbreaking situation to which they are subjected during their earthly pilgrimage. They cannot forget that they are traveling through a strange land, walking in search of their Homeland: *There is no permanent city for us here; we are looking for the one which is yet to be.*[6] Considering this problem from a superficial point of view, and even more so if one dispenses with faith, one may think that Christians live in a condition of existential schizophrenia: on the one hand, they must live in the world with all its consequences and face every kind of situation; on the other, they must become, at the same time, completely oblivious to their surroundings, as though indifferent to them. As the Apostle said in regard to this last point: *But I say this brethren, the time is short; it remaineth, that they that have wives be as though they had none; and they that weep, as though they wept not; and they that rejoice, as*

---

[4]Phil 1: 23–24.
[5]Col 3: 1–2.
[6]Heb 13:14.

though they rejoiced not; and they that buy, as though they possessed not; and they that use this world, as not abusing it; for the fashion of this world passeth away.[7] Are we then dealing with an aporia of two antagonistic situations which are unsustainable in their mutual opposition...?

The rice plant grows in hot climates and in swampy or flooded lands, so it is said that the plant likes to have its feet in the water and its head in the fire. The Christian position is not based on two contradictory foundations: *it is one of balance between seemingly opposing but, in fact, complementary situations.* And as always happens with any equilibrium, it is maintained with difficulty. It should be remembered that no one has ever said that Christian life is easy or comfortable. Both situations are complementary because the human being is both matter and spirit; put to the test as he walks along a path between two worlds —Heaven and Earth— to which he belongs at one and the same time, he does need to prove his faith and to participate in the sufferings and death of his Lord.

Hence the Christian should tread the earth with his feet set firmly upon it in order to share the problems of his brothers..., while, at the same time, keeping his heart in Heaven, his true Homeland, toward which he walks tire-

---

[7] 1 Cor 7: 29–31.

lessly. No one can ever say that either of the two positions ceases to matter to the other, since they are mutually complementary and essential: entry into the promised Homeland that is Heaven, for example, depends on how well one has accomplished his journey on Earth; and a fruitful stay on Earth, fully exploiting its contingencies, circumstances, and problems (one's own and those of other men, one's brothers), is necessarily linked to the fact that one was able to elevate his heart to Heaven.

At any rate, the earthly journey turns out smooth and even beautiful when the heart is nostalgic for its Lord Whose memory fills the existence of the disciple with the sure hope that one day, finally, the Road will come to an end. Then *there shall be no more death, neither sorrow, nor crying, neither shall there be any more pain: for the former things are passed away;*[8] there the disciple in love with his Lord will have definitively arrived;

> *And there at the end of the road we will find,*
> *Our toils and hard labors are left far behind.*[9]

---

[8] Rev 21:4.

[9] *CFC*, n. 2. In the Spanish original: *allí donde se acaba la vereda/ y el duro trajinar atrás se queda.*

It will be there, and only there, that the bride will finally hear clearly the voice of her Bridegroom. And there she will be united forever with Him for Whom her restless and wounded heart had been looking for a lifetime:

> *And there my ended woes and sorrows left me*
> *There where our lives are joined as one, by the sea*
> *Rocked with gentle waves created easily*
> *By the stirred blue waters lapping lazily.*[10]

---

[10] *CFC*, n. 105. In the Spanish original: *Y allí mis penas fueron fenecidas/ junto al mar que vio unidas nuestras vidas,/ mecido en suaves ondas, producidas/ por las azules aguas removidas.*

VII

At night he left for the distant mountain range,
At night he walked on the road around the bend,
At night I was left in foreign lands and strange,
At night I was found alone without my friend.[1]

Ever since Jesus Christ ascended into Heaven in the presence of His Apostles and disciples, Christians have shed tears because of His absence and felt a deep longing for His presence, while at the same time they have been comforted by the hope of His promised Return. Centuries and even millennia have passed, and the disciples who still persevere are overwhelmed with the sadness of

---

[1] *CFC*, n. 23. In the Spanish original: *De noche se marchó hacia la montaña,/ de noche se perdió por el sendero,/ de noche me dejó por tierra extraña,/ de noche me encontré sin compañero.*

feeling abandoned, while they are sustained by an intense longing to see Him again.

In the beginning, the primitive Community was convinced that His Return was merely a matter of days, possibly months, but not much more than that. As time went by, what happened to the Virgins of the Parable was also experienced by the disciples: they fell into despair, and their remembrance of the Lord became increasingly diminished.

For He tarried too long: *While the bridegroom tarried, they slumbered and slept.*[2] Today, only a small number of disciples are still waiting; they form isolated groups, increasingly smaller and less numerous, as the world intensifies its persecution against them. And, as if this were not enough, they live overwhelmed, anxious because of the warning uttered by their Master that the worst is yet to come: *But when the Son of man cometh, shall he find faith on the earth?*[3]

Of course, given the present situation afflicting the World and the Church, it is not surprising that those who still remain faithful live burdened with the sadness caused by the absence of their Lord. Sorrow which, incidentally,

---

[2] Mt 25:5.
[3] Lk 18:8.

He had already foretold on the Night of His Farewell Supper: *Now I go my way to him who sent me; and none of you asketh me, Whither goest thou? But because I have said these things unto you, sorrow hath filled your heart. Nevertheless I tell you the truth; It is expedient for you that I go away...*[4] Earlier He had warned: *Little children, yet a little while I am with you. Ye shall seek me, and, as I said unto the Jews, Whither I go, ye cannot come; so now I say to you.*[5]

Leon Bloy said that there is but one sadness, not to be saints. Actually, one may speak of a greater sorrow still: the effect of the absence of Our Lord. Anything else that may happen to a Christian cannot be for him any cause for anguish because all things work together for good to them that love God (Rom 8:28).

The bride in the *Song of Songs* laments bitterly that she cannot find the Bridegroom, and so she longingly seeks Him in the middle of the night; night is indeed for a Christian any situation in which Jesus Christ seems to have disappeared: *Because the night cometh, when no man can work.*[6] And what can be done when the absence of the

---

[4] Jn 16: 5–7.

[5] Jn 13:33.

[6] Jn 9:4.

Bridegroom turns everything into a *Dark Night* in which life seems to have been deprived of all meaning?:

> *By night on my bed*
> *I sought him whom my soul loveth:*
> *I sought him, but I found him not.*
> *I will rise now, and go about the city in the streets,*
> *And in the broad ways*
> *I will seek him whom my soul loveth.*[7]

Where can one go when it seems that the world has lost all faith and that even the Church has come to believe that man —his dignity, his rights— is the only thing truly important?

Can anyone imagine a more painful situation than one in which the Church and the World seem to have lost sight of Jesus and no longer know a way to find Him? *Woman, why weepest thou?* —the angels at the empty tomb asked Mary Magdalene— *Because they have taken away my Lord, and I know not where they have laid him,* she said.[8]

Is the Pilgrim Church now in the final and most difficult stage of her History, which is precisely the period

---

[7] Sg 3: 1–2.
[8] Jn 20:13.

referred to in the prophecies as the End of Time? Is the difficult time already at hand when even the elect, feeling isolated and abandoned in the midst of a godless world, are also in danger of doubting their faith (Mt 24:24)? It is because Darkness has descended upon the World that it can no longer find Jesus Christ:

> *In the dark of night my Beloved left me,*
> *As the sun drops past the hills into the west,*
> *As the broad river flows into the wide sea,*
> *And the fleeting stag runs into the forest.*[9]

However, the true disciple of Jesus will never see his hope disappointed: *We glory in tribulations also, knowing that tribulation worketh patience; and patience, tested virtue; and tested virtue, hope. And hope does not let us down.*[10] Finally, in the end, when everything seems lost, we will hear again in the distance the low whistle of the Shepherd who leads us to where He is:

---

[9] *CFC*, n. 22. In the Spanish original: *De noche se marchó el Amado mío,/ como se oculta el sol tras el collado,/ cual se pierde en el mar el ancho río/ y en los espesos bosques el venado.*

[10] Rom 5: 3–5.

In your orchard a small bird,
In grief at your absence, sang with a sad sound;
And, when your soft voice she heard,
Quickly rose up from the ground,
To search in her swift flight where you could be found.[11]

---

[11] *CFC*, n. 9. In the Spanish original: *De tu vergel un ave/ por tu ausencia cantaba en desconsuelo;/ y oyó tu voz suave,/ y, alzándose del suelo,/ a buscarte emprendió veloz su vuelo.*

VIII

In the peaceful calm of night
Of the silent, wooded valley without gloom,
With deep, sweet pain, now so right,
The waiting for the Bridegroom
Fills the soul with ardent, impatient delight.[1]

The Cinderella of the three theological virtues is Hope: the least known, the least talked about, and generally considered as the least important virtue of the three. However, these virtues form such a unity that should one of them be missing, the other two would disappear. Saint

---

[1] *CFC.* n. 108. In the Spanish original: *En la noche serena/ del silencioso valle nemoroso,/ en honda y dulce pena,/ la espera del Esposo/ de ardorosa impaciencia mi alma llena.*

Paul catalogs them simply as *the three virtues*, recognizing that they form a homogeneous and compact whole — although he ascribes to charity the most important status (1 Cor 13:13).

In the Christian's present state of pilgrimage toward his Homeland (Heb 13:14), Charity would be meaningless without the virtue of Hope —its existence would not even be imaginable. The same can be said about Hope in regard to the absence of Charity, or about Faith with respect to either of the other two.

It is true, however, that once the Road has ended and the Heavenly Jerusalem is reached at last, only Charity remains in that blessed existence (1 Cor 13:8). *For the hope that is seen is not hope: For what a man seeth, why doth he hope for?*[2] But, until that time, Hope gives the full meaning and provides the necessary encouragement for our pilgrimage through the Valley of Tears. Indeed, whereto would the Christian be walking without it...? And without Hope, what value could be attributed to our earthly existence as we travel over this narrow, steep, and difficult path (Mt 7:14), not knowing where we are going or even why we must make such an arduous trek...? Therefore, without the virtue of Hope, any possibility of a Christian

---

[2]Rom 8:24.

life would fade away; this life would no longer have any meaning: *If our hope in Christ has been for this life only, we are of all men the most miserable.*[3] Hence the stanza:

> *In her flight toward the hill, her anguish a knife,*
> *Sorely wounded by love, the bird seeks for him*
> *Who was her companion, her partner for life;*
> *But seeing her hopes dashed, her prospects now grim,*
> *She lay on the path, and death ended the strife.*[4]

In the early fifties of the last century, Samuel Beckett published his tragicomedy *Waiting for Godot*, which belongs to the literary genre *theater of the absurd*. This existentialist play seeks to portray the complete meaninglessness of human life. Its two characters, Vladimir and Estragon, wait endlessly and in vain for the arrival of someone named Godot. Although the author denied any reference to God in the name of his awaited character, Godot, it is clear that his nihilistic intention was to suggest the supreme human absurdity of waiting for a

---

[3] 1 Cor 15:19.

[4] *CFC*. n. 26. In the Spanish original: *En vacilante vuelo y derrotero,/ busca un ave, de amores malherida,/ al que fue de su vida el compañero,/ mas viendo su esperanza ya perdida,/ muerta quedó tendida en el sendero.*

promised God who does not arrive and never will. This is how the play was widely interpreted.

Back in the realm of correct approach we see that, according to Saint Paul, absence of true Christian Hope makes the Christian the most miserable of all men. Of course, Existentialism, always attracted by the mysterious abyss of *non–being*, goes even further and indicates that despair diminishes man, reducing him to a hopeless being doomed to nothingness and subjected to a type of ephemeral and meaningless existence.

Still, the creature has not yet come to understand what happens when Hope is lost: the tragedy that follows as a result of lost Hope surpasses all that can be imagined by the human mind. It is not only that the loss of Hope reduces man to the status of a *being for naught*, as Existentialism contends; now man becomes a creature condemned to eternal despair in whose heart any glimmer of hope is gone. Not surprisingly, Dante placed this inscription on the frontispiece of the Gateway to Hell:

> *Through me the way is to the city dolent;*
> *Through me the way is to eternal dole;*
> *Through me the way among the people lost.*

Justice incited my sublime Creator;
Created me divine Omnipotence,
The highest Wisdom and the primal Love.

Before me there were no created things,
Only eterne, and I eternal last.
All hope abandon, ye who enter in![5]

As we have said, Hope has vanished from the Dolent City, which lasts forever and from which all hint of Love has been banished; Hope will never again appear in the constant succession of centuries which, in the time–without–time of Eternity, knows no stop or end.

It is true that the Virtue of Hope comes from above, but it also garners strength from the hardships and sufferings that the disciple of Jesus encounters throughout his lifetime. For Hope gives meaning to those trials and transforms them into fruits of Eternity; this virtue is also the main cause of the Joy that fills the Christian life, as noted by the Apostle Saint Paul: *We glory in tribulations also, knowing that tribulation worketh patience; and patience, tested virtue; and tested virtue, hope. And hope does not let us down because the love of God is poured out into our hearts, by the Holy Ghost, who is given to us.*[6]

---

[5] Dante, *Divine Comedy*, Inferno, Canto III.
[6] Rom 5: 3–5.

Therefore, because of one of those paradoxes whose deepest reason only God knows, Hope, contrary to popular belief, far from *being merely* a *virtue of consolation*, is intended to flood with joy the voyage that the Christian must undertake on his journey Homeward. An exciting itinerary which normally passes, as we have said, along a narrow and rough path; and yet, at the same time, this journey acquires the characteristic proper to the Way of Perfect Joy.

IX

Loving Dialogue.

Within this issue, speaking of a *Loving Dialogue* would be a tautology or to say it more clearly, a redundancy; for any true dialogue is a loving dialogue. Any relationship between rational beings —whether between Creator and His creatures or between created ones and their Creator or, among creatures, between two individual persons— necessarily takes place within the framework of a *loving relationship*; consequently, that relationship cannot ever happen but through love itself.

All creatures are a reflection of the divine perfections, which they participate in to a greater or lesser degree. There can be no relationship worthy of that name among rational creatures which does not involve an analogy that resembles the loving relationships within the Trinity.[1]

The Word, spoken by the Father about Himself and for Himself by the Father from all Eternity, begets the Person of the Son: the comprehensive, all–encompassing Response given *at the same instant* in one timeless, eternal moment (intellectual generation). The Person of the Son, in turn, corresponds with the reply of a loving *Yes* to the Father: the perfect, absolute *Yes* Who, along with the immanent operation of the Father, constitutes the Person of the Holy Spirit as the loving and reciprocal *spiration* of both the Son and the Father (active and passive spiration). Wherefore, God is Love because He is the loving Dialogue between separate Persons (in one and only Divine Essence). From then on, every true dialogue which, after all, is but a reflection and participation —like the whole of creation— in the perfections of God, cannot be but a loving dialogue.

---

[1]There exist in the Holy Trinity four real relations among the Three Persons: fatherhood, sonship, passive spiration, and active spiration. Only three of them stand in opposition to one another and, therefore, are really distinct: fatherhood, sonship, and passive spiration. Active spiration is in opposition only to passive spiration but not to fatherhood and sonship and, therefore, is only virtually distinct from them. Hence the Trinity of Persons, who are really distinct from one another although each one is identical to the Unique, Simple Divine Essence.

According to this, all dialogue is the expression of a relationship of love. For that and for no other purpose has God granted man the gift of speech and the ability to communicate. Within the Trinity, the Word responded with an absolute *Yes,* which implies a perfect *relationship of love* between the Divine Persons; from that moment on, every word uttered by God to His creatures, or by them to Him, or among themselves, would become meaningless if the utterance does not become a vehicle for expressing *a relationship of love.*

Actually, language is distorted when it is no longer used as a vehicle to express love. Attributing any other meaning to language is an aberration in that it contradicts the natural order established by God's plan, by which and for which He created His rational creatures. Every word uttered out of this context is uttered in vain: *I tell you that every idle word that men shall speak, they shall render an account for it on the Day of Judgment. For by thy words thou shalt be justified, and by thy words thou shalt be condemned.*[2]

God has never spoken to man *except to express His love for him.* Hence His Word is warm and sweet and soft as well as peremptory; as acknowledged so well in this verse:

---

[2]Mt 12: 36–37.

My Bridegroom's voice is for me,
Like the wake of a ship deeply furrowing
Like winds that stir so lightly
Like a gentle whispering,
Like the solemn moves of a night bird on wing.[3]

At the same time the Word is cutting, sharp, and effective, penetrating the deepest recesses of soul and heart. For love is like this... and even more so when it is Perfect, Infinite Love Who gives Himself and speaks: *The Word of God is living and effectual, and more penetrating than any two-edged sword: reaching unto the division of the soul and the spirit, of the joints also, and the marrow, and is a discerner of the thoughts and intents of the heart.*[4]

It could not be otherwise, for love is at the pole most opposite to superficiality, lack of totality, temporality; hence love does not understand terms or conditions, but only the totality and eternity of the absolute. This is how the *Song of Songs* describes it, using poetic and expressive metaphors suited to human understanding:

---

[3]*CFC*, n. 75. In the Spanish original: *Es la voz del Esposo/ como la huidiza estela de una nave,/ como aire rumoroso,/ como susurro suave,/ como el vuelo nocturno de algún ave.*

[4]Heb 4:12.

For love is as strong as death,
Jealousy as cruel as the grave;
Its flames are flames of fire,
A flame of Yahweh.
Many waters cannot quench love,
Nor can the floods drown it.[5]

As can be seen, we are at the antipodes to the way the World understands Dialogue... including many theologians and pastoral experts within the Church. Is *Ecumenical Dialogue* really a means for union among Churches? Does it really qualify as true Dialogue? Dialogues are not intended to reach *a neutral point of encounter*; on the contrary, they cannot claim any purpose other than reaching *the center, the very place where true love abides*, as we have said. Therefore, everything seems to indicate that when Christians are willing to comply with the New Commandment issued by the Master on the Night of the Last Supper — practicing a mutual and reciprocal love—, only then will the desired goal of having one Flock and one Shepherd be achieved (Jn 10:16).

But love happens to be a feeling so immensely serious as to be dealt with here according to its true meaning,

---

[5]Sg 8: 6–7.

even as jealousy: *The Lord your God is a consuming fire and a jealous God.*[6]

It is a great misfortune that man does not quite understand that God is even more longing than man himself to hear the voice of His creature uttering a loving and affirmative response to His love. In fact, He does not even know how to convey His greatest yearnings when He addresses man; for He is bound to express Himself through the poor and limited means of human words:

> *My Love's voice is a sweet sigh*
> *As when the turtledove breathes her low soft coo;*
> *Like a new rose-colored sky*
> *Rich with multicolored hue*
> *When at last the rising sun comes into view.*[7]

---

[6] Deut 4:24.

[7] *CFC,* n. 74. In the Spanish original: *Es la voz de la amada/ como un arrullo dulce de paloma,/ como un alba rosada/ que mil colores toma/ cuando el sol por los montes ya se asoma.*

X

The time for love.

The Psalmist already noted that *fear of the Lord is the beginning of wisdom.*[1] But the notion of fear was not at all part of the First Plan of God concerning His intercourse with men. Fear, except when it is simply a natural reaction caused by our instinct for self–preservation, is but an anomaly of human nature, a product of sin; which is, in turn, the worst aberration that the rational creature can bring upon himself:

And the Lord God called unto Adam, and said unto him, Where art thou? And he said, I heard thy voice in

---

[1] Ps 111:10.

the garden, and I was afraid, because I was naked; and I hid myself.[2]

Love and fear are incompatible, as the Apostle Saint John said. And God has always wished to maintain relations of perfect love with man:

There is no fear in love; but perfect love casteth out fear; because fear hath torment. He that feareth is not made perfect in love.[3]

Hence the need, in the new order inaugurated by the New Covenant, that the dialogue between man and God should resume the normal mutual relationship contemplated in the Original Plan; in truth, improvement was even inevitable with respect to the first condition, because now, thanks to Jesus Christ, man can talk with God *face–to–face*, or as equals, since God Himself became Man. Enmity has been transformed forever into love; the *Old Man* has been definitively replaced by the *New Man* (Eph 2:15) whose *novelty* reaches beyond the old Adam. For it must be noted that Christ, from the moment of His Incarnation, is also the Lord of Time; through Him all things are reconciled unto Himself (Col 1: 15–20).

---

[2]Gen 3: 9–10.

[3]1 Jn 4:18

And so the *newness* that He brought with Him surpasses the *first novelty* of the moment of Creation before the Fall. His *new commandment* is so original that one can rightly conclude that its rich and deep content, far from being a return to the beginning, had never before been promulgated or even heard of by men after so many millennia in the History of the World. The truth is that the *novelty* of the new commandment has not been sufficiently emphasized; rather we tend to regard it as a confirmation of the first commandment of the Decalogue. But we ought to presume that, since Jesus Christ calls it *new*, we need to consider it a true *innovation* whose content transcends and surpasses completely the requirements of the first precept. Therefore, it can be very well said that Christ has made both *the past* and *the future* present in His Person, renewing both of them.

So, looking back to Time already elapsed, one could say:

Therefore if any man be in Christ, he is a new creature: old things are passed away; behold, all things are made new.[4]

And, looking forward to the succession of eons that cover both the present and the future, one can also say:

---

[4] 2 Cor 5:17.

And he that sat upon the throne said, Behold, I make all things new.[5]

That is why it was proclaimed to the whole created Universe, as a solemn proof:

Jesus Christ the same yesterday and today and forever.[6]

For Love not only exists before all Time, He is also able to transcend and reach beyond Time. And because man has been made partaker of Perfect Love through Jesus Christ, it is clear that he has also been granted the likeness of Eternity.

And so the time for love has come again. And, with it, old songs of love once more are heard, whose echoes have been resounding through mountains and hills, repeated then through shady forests and lush meadows, until they come down to the sea and are mixed with the murmuring of the waves. Now it is not a restored love, but a new and more beautiful one, as it always happens with every dawn; and with the flowers which appear each spring and offer to the senses a new and resplendent beauty, more intense than the beauty of the ones which delighted men of other

---

[5] Rev 21:5.
[6] Heb 13:8.

eras gone by with their color and perfume. For every love is always new.

> *I will join you there, my Love,*
> *On the misty slopes of craggy mountains deep*
> *Near foxes' dens and above,*
> *Silver summits tower steep*
> *In the silence of forgotten snows we keep...*
>
> *We will stay there, high above,*
> *And sing together the blissful songs of love.*[7]

Thus, the *newness of now*, provided by Christ, far exceeds the *primeval novelty* at the time of Creation; for we have been told by the Apostle that *where sin abounded, grace did much more abound* (Rom 5:20). Therefore, the *new commandment*, far from being a return to the beginning, is so original that it had never been enacted, nor has its full content and meaning hitherto ever been known: *For in Christ Jesus neither circumcision availeth anything, nor uncircumcision, but a new creature.*[8]

---

[7] *CFC*. n. 72. In the Spanish original: *Amado, en las brumosas/ laderas de montañas escarpadas,/ con cuevas de raposas/ y cimas plateadas/ en silencio de nieves olvidadas...// Allí nos estaremos/ y los cantos de amor entonaremos.*

[8] Gal 6:15.

For indeed, the new time to love is finally come again, though now under the proper form of *perfect love*, never known before by any man, after so many millennia in the History of the World have already passed:

> *When night has shed her mantle of mystery*
> *And daybreak dawns, followed by a rosy sky,*
> *I run to the flowery meadow eagerly*
> *To meet again my Loved One, and he with me.*
> *For sweet hour has come at last and brings a sigh;*
> *And the time for love has arrived finally.*[9]

And the Voice of God is neither vindictive nor threatening with punishments but sweet and loving; even humble and pleading, at least for those who want to hear it, as it often happens with the enticing repartee of any lover:

Behold, I stand at the door, and knock: if any man shall hear my voice and open the door, I will come in to him, and will sup with him, and he with me.[10]

---

[9] *CFC*, n. 85. In the Spanish original: *Pues ya la Noche el manto ha abandonado,/ y al alba sigue la rosada aurora,/ ansioso corro hasta el florido prado/ en impaciente busca del Amado,/ después de que sonó la dulce hora/ en que el tiempo de amar es ya llegado.*

[10] Rev 3:20.

XI

True dialogue and silence.

Even men of good will who truly love God tend to think that in prayer He merely listens. The truth is, however, that, since God has chosen to establish a relationship of true love with man, divine–human dialogue is essential to those relationships; hence the need for prayer.

But few Christians understand that prayer is not just a monologue on their part, presenting requests or giving thanks in the hope of being heard; far from that. Prayer is a true dialogue, and even more; for the relation of love can be expressed in various ways that go beyond a simple exchange of words, as the bride of the *Song of Songs* already said:

His left arm is under my head,
His right embraces me.[1]

After the Ascension of Our Lord into Heaven, the customary way of achieving divine–human dialogue takes place through and in Jesus Christ through the Spirit: *These things have I spoken unto you, being yet present with you. But the Paraclete, the Holy Ghost, whom the Father will send in my name, he shall teach you all things, and bring all things to your remembrance, whatsoever I have said unto you.*[2]

In the history of Christian spirituality there have been many who have tried to maintain some sort of communication with the Spirit, following a trend that has increased of late. In modern times, *Charismatic Movements* and similar groups are the ones that most often lay claim to His assistance. But this belief is impossible to confirm or deny because all official Revelation was closed upon the death of the last Apostle; consequently, *only the Magisterium of the Church, when speaking in the imperative form of infallibility*, is the sole guarantor of trustworthiness concerning the inspirations of the Spirit.

---

[1] Sg 2:6.
[2] Jn 14: 25–26.

And since it is not easy to attribute authenticity to the unofficial assistance of the Spirit —in addition to the real possibility, confirmed in many cases, of being deceived by the Devil's work—, mystics and spiritual writers have developed an extensive and complex doctrine of the so–called *discretion* or *discernment of spirits*, in an attempt to distinguish between the impulses of the good and the evil spirit. Be this as it may, it is clear that the Spirit of God has a very peculiar and unique way of addressing man, which unfortunately is not always taken into account. We are referring to simple *references* that are to be considered regarding His communications and whose presence or absence can lead, somehow, to acquiring a *relative* certainty regarding the authenticity of those communications.

For example, the Spirit is modest and is partial to discretion and silence. On the other hand, He hates publicity, pomp, noise, or reference to His Person when someone, who boldly and without any grounds other than his own arrogance, seeks to validate his own actions or doctrines with those despised elements. Usually, when someone proclaims from the rooftops that he speaks or acts at the bidding of the Spirit, we can say almost certainly that he is speaking of his own accord. The real movements of the Spirit often go unnoticed, except by those to whom they are directed, in that they are always accompanied by humility, modesty, and simplicity: as notes that are peculiar to genuine holiness.

Any discreet man would not give credence to alleged acts of the Spirit done with exhibition. Looking after one's own protagonism, always covertly and with poorly disguised pretensions of holiness, is incompatible with the modes of action of the Spirit Who does not seem to be willing to lend Himself to be invoked at will, as if He were the genie of Aladdin's lamp: *Where the Spirit of the Lord is, there is liberty...*[3] And as to the criteria used by God to deliver His gifts, especially His charisms, they are as incomprehensible as they are unknown to human beings. As God told the prophet Elijah:

Then he was told, 'Go out and stand on the mountain before Yahweh.' For at that moment Yahweh was going by. A mighty hurricane split the mountains and shattered the rocks before Yahweh. But Yahweh was not in the hurricane. And after the hurricane, an earthquake. But Yahweh was not in the earthquake. And after the earthquake, fire. But Yahweh was not in the fire. And after the fire, a light murmuring sound. And when Elijah heard this, he covered his face with his cloak and went out and

---

[3] 2 Cor 3:17.

stood at the entrance of the cave. Then a voice came to him, which said, 'What are you doing here, Elijah?'[4]

The Voice of God does not usually desire noise or advertising with its air of aggrandizement or clapping of hands. Even the murmuring of the wind seems to stop and listen to that Voice:

> *When dawn is still soft, before the morning sun,*
> *In misty valleys amid cliffs dyed with dew*
> *The apple exudes her perfumed elation*
> *And in the far distance the turtle doves coo,*
> *You beckon your bride, your sister, your dear one*
> *With the ancient echoes of songs old and true.*
> *And as the wind pauses its wailings to hear,*
> *Your sighings and wooings are brought to my ear.*[5]

Current Catholicism, too much inclined to have its voice taken into account by the World, has turned to and adopted a barrage of advertising resources: proclamations, discourses, exhortations, speeches, addresses, workshops,

---

[4] 1 Kings 19: 11–13.

[5] *CFC*, n. 36. In the Spanish original: *Cuando el alba suave aún no es mañana/ y en el valle florido, entre los tejos,/ exhala sus fragancias la manzana/ y se arrulla la tórtola a lo lejos,/ Tú clamas por tu esposa, por tu hermana,/ con eco antiguo de cantares viejos.../ Y el viento hace una pausa en sus gemidos/ trayendo tu reclamo a mis oídos.*

conferences..., and new and modern methods for shepherd-
ing souls. These procedures assert to be a vehicle for the
Voice of God or an echo of His teachings; unfortunately,
their content is more often than not, pure wind —thus the
ancient revelation of Elijah is brought up–to–date: *The
Lord was not in the wind.* They indeed sound like hol-
low voices, stirring up confusion rather than trust. By
contrast, the Good Shepherd *goes before his sheep and
the sheep follow him because they know his voice. But a
stranger they follow not, but flee from him, because they
know not the voice of strangers.*[6]

The Spirit is the Love of God, and He utilizes His own
language, spoken in His own way, as we have just said.
That is why the dialogue of true lovers takes place within
the intimacy of silence:

> *Following shepherds and sheep,*
> *I came to where the Loved One awaited me*
> *Hidden in hillsides so deep;*
> *As he spoke to me softly*
> *The whistling sounds of the jungle ceased to be.*[7]

---

[6] Jn 10: 4–5.

[7] *CFC,* n. 6. In the Spanish original: *Siguiendo a los pastores/
busqué donde el Amado me esperaba/ oculto en los alcores./ Y al tiempo
que me hablaba/ el susurro del viento se escuchaba.*

In the Church —and only in the Church— the Spirit speaks to men through the authoritative voice of the authentic and legitimate Magisterium. He has never failed in His words nor has He ever contradicted Himself. As we have said, He is Sovereign Freedom (2 Cor 3:17), working where He wants and being bound only to Himself. Hence one can assume that they are too daring who claim that they can conjure Him at will and that they are receptive channels of His inspirations. But reality does not work that way because: *The Spirit breatheth where he will, and thou hearest his voice; but thou knowest not whence he cometh, nor whither he goeth.*[8]

Indeed, for who can know where Love comes from and whither He leads...? We can hear His Voice; but who can claim to have comprehended the unfathomable, deep content of that Voice? And who has ever been able to explain, to the extent required by the cravings of the human heart, what Love is?

---

[8] Jn 3:8.

XII

If you should see me again,
Down in the glen where the singing blackbirds fly,
Do not say you love me then
For, were you ever to repeat that sweet sigh,
On hearing it, I may die.[1]

Everyone will agree that this lyre, which was originally part of a mystical composition, can be applied, on different levels, to both divine–human love and purely human love. Nevertheless, it should be noted that some clarifications would be necessary before accepting this equation.

As anyone can see at once, this lyric poem refers to love in its purest and most noble form. It is a difficult

---

[1] *CFC.* n. 52. In the Spanish original: *Si de nuevo me vieres,/ allá en el valle, donde canta el mirlo,/ no digas que me quieres,/ no muera yo al oírlo/ si acaso tú volvieras a decirlo.*

task; the poem uses the expressive power of the mysterious phrase *I love you*: an expression understood and used by everyone, but whose deepest meaning nobody has ever clarified. It is true that anyone who hears it or utters it clearly understands what it tries to convey, but he does not have the capacity to grasp its deepest significance. In fact, *no one* has been able yet to penetrate the mystery it holds, much less explain it completely.

Nevertheless, we can say that a serious consideration of this issue soon reveals that it is *extremely difficult* to apply this expression to purely human love... unless we are willing to be satisfied —as it normally happens— with merely attributing to this phrase the very meaning which simple words contain; they either express feelings too poor in substance or are just one of the many conventions embraced by deception when applied to this case.

This said, it could be affirmed that we are getting near the heart of the issue; for we are facing, although no one may want to admit it, the most serious problem afflicting Humanity today. We refer to the alarming fact that men *have lost sight of the concept of Love.* Love has been too frequently reduced either to what is now understood as *sex* in the way that millions of human beings think of it or to a notion which merely expresses superficial feelings devoid of content and having little or nothing to do with the fundamental attributes of love: total, unconditional, faithful, and everlasting.

Although Christians themselves rarely realize this problem, it is a proven fact that, since Catholics started walking along the new path designated for them by the Second Vatican Council, the Church barely speaks of love. In terms of human love, this notion has been replaced by that of *solidarity*; as for love due to God, it has been reduced to an extinct species, characteristic of earlier times, when Christians still thought affectionately of God and addressed themselves to Him trusting in His infinite Goodness.

Moreover, the phrase *I love you*, when referring to a purely human love relationship, falls short in terms of expressing the content and meaning of that love. Because, unlike what happens with divine–human love, merely human love (even pure love, elevated by grace) expresses itself by means of ideas and words that, even being honest and true to their significance, are, however, not able to express the reality to which they refer in all its depth. Merely human love must resort to metaphors and other language–related resources in order to configure a set of simple desires which will hardly go beyond just that, desires. Expressions such as *my life, my heart, totally yours,* and the like, even when their sincerity cannot be doubted, are nothing more than attempts and aspirations that will never go far beyond *I wish I could, but I cannot.*

In the lyre we are commenting, the enamoured person tells her beloved not to address her with the expression *I love you*, or at least not to repeat it. The lover warns the beloved of the danger of her dying if she should hear it again. But, is it possible that the feeling roused by love could be so strong...? A qualifying answer should distinguish: of course not, if we are referring to love that is often commonly known as such; but indeed yes, if we are dealing with true love.

> *For love is strong as Death,*
> *Passion as relentless as Sheol.*
> *The flash of it is a flash of fire,*
> *A flame of Yahweh himself.*[2]

So much so that Christian death makes no sense unless it is out of love: *For none of us liveth to himself; and no man dieth to himself. For whether we live, we live unto the Lord; or whether we die, we die unto the Lord.*[3] If the Christian does not die to himself but unto the Lord,

---

[2]Sg 8:6.

[3]Rom 14: 7–8.

how else can it be said that his death is death out of love?
Hence this stanza:

> *At early dawn still rosy*
> *I searched the thickets of the woods with great pace.*
> *For Him Who enamours me*
> *With the splendor of His face;*
> *As he compels me to meet Him at great haste.*[4]

And this other, in regard to the said consequences that
true love can cause:

> *In flight toward the hill, her uneasiness rife,*
> *Sorely wounded by love, the bird seeks for him*
> *Who was her companion, her partner for life;*
> *But seeing her hopes dashed, her prospects grow grim*
> *She lay on the path, and death ended the strife.*[5]

---

[4] *CFC*, n. 89. In the Spanish original: *En la rosada aurora/ salí a buscar, del bosque en la espesura,/ a Aquél que me enamora,/ que me azara en rubor por su hermosura/ y que corra a su encuentro me apresura.*

[5] *CFC* n. 26. In the Spanish original: *En vacilante vuelo y derrotero,/ busca un ave, de amores malherida,/ al que fue de su vida el compañero,/ mas viendo su esperanza ya perdida,/ muerta quedó tendida en el sendero.*

XIII

If you should see me again,
Down in the glen where the singing blackbirds fly,
Do not say you love me then
For, were you ever to repeat that sweet sigh,
On hearing it, I may die.[1]

The ways which human love uses to express itself, although sincere and emanating from the depths of the heart, can hardly exceed the field of figurative language. Common expressions and sayings in human love relationships such as *my life, my heart, all and always yours, two in one soul,* or the like, do not go beyond mere symbolism.

---

[1] *CFC,* n. 52. In the Spanish original: *Si de nuevo me vieres,/ allá en el valle, donde canta el mirlo,/ no digas que me quieres,/ no muera yo al oírlo/ si acaso tú volvieras a decirlo.*

The very act of love that takes place in conjugal union, by which both spouses become *one flesh* as the Bible says,[2] is but an attempt to *merge lives and attain a mutual possession* that never fulfills all that it hopes to be.

In the relationship of divine–human love things happen in a very different manner. Here one no longer deals with metaphors but with true realities, even though the depth of their substance remains shrouded during this life in the most unfathomable mystery: *He who eats my flesh and drinks my blood 'abides in me and I in him.' As the living Father has sent me, and I live by the Father, 'so he that eats me shall live because of me.'*[3] It should be noted here that Jesus Christ establishes an equivalence between His life and that of the Father, on the one hand, and His own life and the life of him who eats His flesh, on the other. And elsewhere: *I am the living bread which came down from heaven. If any man eat of this bread, he shall live forever; and the bread that I will give is my flesh for the life of the world.*[4] The ideas put forward by Saint Paul in this regard are as mysterious as they are deeply expressive — and even baffling: *I live, yet no longer I, but Christ lives in*

---

[2] Mt 19:6.

[3] Jn 6: 56–57.

[4] Jn 6:51.

me...[5] *Every one of you who has been baptized into Christ 'has put on Christ'*;[6] etc.

The first thing to be noted about these expressions is that they are based upon *realities* which have nothing to do with metaphor or symbolism; what we have here is a real transfusion of two lives, in which we should say that each one, rather than interchanging his life, *makes the life of the other his own life* while maintaining his own identity. This transfusion does not mean here *fusion* or transformation of two persons into only one or of one person into the other; which would be an aberrant belief leading directly to pantheism.

For in the divine–human love relationship, each of the lovers keeps intact his own person and his own specific identity; otherwise, the absence of perfect distinction between the two persons who love each other would necessarily preclude the existence of any love *relationship*. The disciple of Jesus Christ makes *his* the life of his Master while still being himself; at the same time, his own life, that is, all his existence, becomes something that belongs to Jesus Christ.

---

[5] Gal 2:20.

[6] Gal 3:27.

When the bride in the *Song of Songs* says, referring to her Bridegroom, that *my Beloved is mine, and I am his*,[7] or *I am my Beloved's, and his desire is for me*,[8] she is using poetic language, for the whole sacred Book is a Poem, but her expressions do describe something that is totally real.

The unfortunate thing about all this is that most believers tend to reduce Christian life to the fulfillment of the commandments, at best. However, within the context of Christian Spirituality, *to put on Christ, live the life of Christ* or, as they say regarding priestly ministry, *be another Christ*, are expressions of a language fully corresponding to reality. He really makes his life the life of Christ who comes to understand these things; in the sense of living the love of his Master, sharing His own thoughts and feelings, making them part of his own existence: *For who hath known the mind of the Lord, that he may instruct him? But we have the mind of Christ.*[9]

In reality, the implications of *making my own* the life of my beloved (and this is not symbolic language) depend on the transcendence given to that person and that love. Now, what happens when that beloved Person is Jesus

---

[7]Sg 1:16.

[8]Sg 7:11.

[9]1 Cor 2:16.

Christ...? Or, vice versa, when someone is the direct object, in the most intimate way, of divine love...? Of course, they cannot know anything about the indescribable joy that comes from divine–human love who reduce love to sex; or those for whom love means nothing more than a merely superficial and fleeting feeling; or even those who have known only purely human love —though dignified and elevated. Jesus was referring to the transcendent effects of the Holy Spirit in the human heart when He said about Him that *the world cannot receive him, because it sees him not, nor knows him.*[10]

According to what has been said, the most mysterious and sweetest of all expressions known to man, the phrase *I love you*, which even in the realm of merely human love is capable of making any heart of flesh quiver with emotion, acquires in divine–human love a peculiar meaning whose deepest content and effects are lost in the unfathomable abyss of God's Heart.

But then, what exactly does the expression *I love you* mean...? What effects might it bring about in the heart of a simple creature when the beloved Person whom he addresses is Jesus? Or when, in perfect reciprocity, this same human creature is the one who hears this expression ut-

---

[10] Jn 14:17.

tered by Him Who also has given His life for him? Or simply when the creature hears it knowing that *it is He Who utters it* and there is no possibility of elaborating further about it? Could anyone understand in all its depth what that death of love referred to in the verse means...?

> *For, were you ever to repeat that sweet sigh,*
> *On hearing it, I may die.*

Anyway, the expression of the bride addressed to her Divine Bridegroom, *I love you*, will not be spoken or heard by her most clearly and in all the depth of its mysterious significance until her arrival Home. Only then will love be fulfilled in all its plenitude, and only then will the human heart feel at last satisfied. In the end, the only one standing will be the one who has lived in accordance with love, because only that will be what counts while everything else is worth nothing.

That is why Saint John of the Cross said that *In the evening of life, you will be judged on love.* Thus, a soul in love with God that is still traveling along the Valley of Tears could also have expressed this same reality, although not with as much poetic inspiration as the Saint, with the following stanza:

The sweet voice that guides me on destiny's way
Leads me through perilous rough roads and inclines,
Now that I envision the close of the day
And softly already the evening star shines.[11]

---

[11] *CFC*, n. 111. In the Spanish original: *La dulce voz que mi destino guía/ por ásperos caminos me conduce,/ hasta que al fin se desvanece el día/ cuando la estrella de la tarde luce.*

XIV

...Do not say you love me then
For, were you ever to repeat that sweet sigh,
On hearing it, I may die.[1]

Is it possible that a declaration of love may impact the listener so strongly as to make him feel faint with love? A prudent response would say that everything depends on the meaning and force attributed to the word *faint*.

As far as purely human (true) love is concerned, expressions such as *dying of love* or *I die because of you, my life*, or similar ones, even when they are pronounced with the greatest sincerity and deepest emotion, are but metaphors only. Lovers such as the characters in the

---

[1]*CFC*, n. 52. In the Spanish original: ...no digas que me quieres,/ no muera yo al oírlo/ si acaso tú volvieras a decirlo.

Shakespearean legend of *Romeo and Juliet* do not die out of love but *because of love*, and also through means that have nothing to do with feelings of love.

In divine–human love, however, things are much more complicated. Here expressions which refer to love and death have implications incomparably stronger than in purely human love and *have little to do with mere metaphor*. Their meaning is tied to *reality*, but cannot be considered on a par with physical or bodily death, from which those expressions clearly distinguish themselves. Phrases like the famous *I die because I do not die* of Saint Teresa of Avila, or the one of Saint Paul that asserts that *I die every day for the glory that you are for me*,[2] and many others of the New Testament are a clear indication of these two different expressions. Mystical spirituality revolves around the idea of death out of love for (in) Jesus Christ. As can be seen, for example in the verses of Saint John of the Cross:

> *O shepherd, you that, yonder,*
> *Go through the sheepfolds of the slope on high,*
> *If you, as there you wander,*
> *Should chance my love to spy,*
> *Then tell him that I suffer, grieve, and die.*[3]

---

[2]1 Cor 15:31.

[3]Saint John of the Cross, *Spiritual Canticle.*

Or these other verses of popular mystical poetry:

> *At early dawn still rosy*
> *I searched the thickets of the woods with great pace,*
> *For Him Who enamours me*
> *With the splendor of His face;*
> *As he compels me to meet Him at great haste.*[4]

The language of the *Song of Songs* tries to convey these facts in an intelligible way to man. The metaphors used by the Sacred Poem are concerned with actualities more than with mere symbolism; actualities that point to a mystery whose depth cannot be perceived by the human creature, though one may get the impression that they refer to the idea of *death* as conceived by man:

> *For love is strong as Death,*
> *Passion as relentless as Sheol.*
> *The flash of it is a flash of fire,*
> *A flame of Yahweh himself.*[5]

---

[4]*CFC*, n. 89. In the Spanish original: *En la rosada aurora/ salí a buscar, del bosque en la espesura,/ a Aquél que me enamora,/ que me azara en rubor por su hermosura/ y que corra a su encuentro me apresura.*

[5]Sg 8:6.

Sometimes, the bride herself admits that she is about to faint because of her love for the Bridegroom.

> *Stay me with raisin cakes,*
> *Comfort me with apples,*
> *For I languish with love.*[6]

Obviously, *languishing* is not yet *dying*; it has to do more with a strong sensation of exhaustion or tiredness that makes man feel as if he were beside himself.

Nevertheless, mystical doctrine does not hesitate to use here the notion of *death* to refer to the effect that *sickness with love* brings about in the human being:

> *Reveal your presence clearly*
> *And kill me with the beauty you discover,*
> *For pains acquired so dearly*
> *From love, cannot recover*
> *Save only through the presence of the lover.*[7]

The same can be said of mystical poetry in general and of the poetry that merely describes profane love, although it is in the former where this notion of dying has its fullest meaning:

---

[6] Sg 2:5.

[7] Saint John of the Cross, *Spiritual Canticle.*

If only in my walking through the valley
By the fir tree forest I could meet with you,
And could contemplate you finally anew,
Death from love I would share with you completely...![8]

But if we admit that the idea of *death out of love* gets its most peculiar significance in mystical doctrine, how can these two concepts of *death* and *love* be reconciled when they are so opposite? If love is identified with life, and Infinite Love, Who is God, is also Infinite Life, then how is it possible to harmonize two realities so radically different as love and death?

The problem arises because of the incorrect, or at least inadequate, application of these two concepts. Even Christians tend to forget that pagan death has nothing to do with the death of the disciples of Jesus Christ —*precious in the eyes of the Lord is the death of his saints*—,[9] for the former is an end, and the latter, by contrast, is a beginning.

Therefore, it is not appropriate to apply the concept of *death* to the final passing away of Christians. The Apostle

---

[8] *CFC*, n. 27. In the Spanish original: *¡Si al recorrer el valle yo pudiera/ en el bosque de abetos encontrarte,/ hasta que al fin de nuevo al contemplarte/ muerte de amor contigo compartiera...!*

[9] Ps 116:15.

Saint John recognizes the incompatibility of both notions when he said that the absence of love is identified with death: *He who loveth not abideth in death.*[10] That is why early Christianity called death of the faithful *dormition*. This is a correct term though not exactly the most fortunate; for it gives rise to the notions of rest, repose, and passivity when, in fact, the arrival Home of the Christian soul and its coming into possession of perfect love involve an act of supreme vitality.

Actually, even the Apostles use the term *dormition* (1 Cor 15:6; 15:18; 1 Thess 4:14; 4:15; 2 Pet 3:4) despite what that act of love means for man. Early Christians used it to refer to the death of the faithful; which is justified if we take into account the practical impossibility of finding another term.[11]

But then, what does the concept of *death out of love* mean exactly and to what extent can it be legitimately used? When the term *death* is used equivocally, it is not

---

[10] 1 Jn 3:14. It follows indirectly from this passage that, for the Evangelist, love and life are identical.

[11] We are dealing here with realities that are part and parcel of the mystery of Christian life and which transcend everything that can be grasped by man's natural knowledge. It is impossible, therefore, to apply any reasonable equivalent notions to these realities.

difficult to see how fitting it is when applied to the effects of love —one of which is the *loss of one's life* so as to give it to the beloved.[12] But what really happens here is very different from what is commonly defined as death of the body with the consequent loss of one's life. What the disciple of Jesus Christ acquires is a state that is precisely the most opposite to that of physical death, for he attains an excess or superabundance of life, given to him specifically by a love in which the words of Jesus Christ become extremely real: *I am come that they might have life, and that they might have it more abundantly.*[13]

This superabundance of life that is the consequence of an overflowing love —and both are the first fruits of the activity of the Holy Ghost (Gal 5:22)— gives rise to an excess of bliss so abundant that it causes in the soul a veritable *languishing* capable of taking away one's life were it not effectively sustained by God; hence the stanza of Saint John of the Cross:

---

[12] *To lose one's life, to give it, or to surrender it out of love* are expressions frequently used in the New Testament (Mt 10:39; 16:25; 20:28; Mk 8:35; Lk 9:24; 17:33; Gal 1:4; 1 Tim 2:6; Tit 2:14; etc.).

[13] Jn 10:10.

> *Oh cautery most tender!*
> *Oh gash that is my guerdon!*
> *Oh gentle hand! Oh touch how softly thrilling!*
> *Eternal life you render,*
> *Raise of all debts the burden*
> *And change my death to life, even while killing!*[14]

Some light is shed upon this mystery when we consider that the follower of Jesus Christ can no longer be subject to death; on the contrary, he becomes the owner and lord of it: *For all things are yours, whether it be Paul or Apollo or Cephas, or the world, or life, or death, or things present, or things to come; all are yours.*[15] This is why the poem says:

> *If living is to love and to be loved so,*
> *My only longing is to live in Love's glow;*
> *If dying is of love to burn in ardor*
> *That consumes the heart, may I quickly die more.*[16]

All these expressions carry a mystical quality which responds to the highest degree of divine–human love and

---

[14] Saint John of the Cross, *O Flame of Love so Living.*

[15] 1 Cor 3: 21–22.

[16] *CFC*, n. 90. In the Spanish original: *Si vivir es amar y ser amado,/ sólo anhelo vivir enamorado;/ si la muerte es de amor ardiente fuego/ que abrasa el corazón, muera yo luego.*

is impossible to be compared to purely human love. They are a poetic, though *absolutely real*, language that puts into words divine–human love as contained in the Bible, especially in the Message of the New Covenant.

Whence is the mysterious power of a declaration of true love? What is the deep and captivating content of the expression *I love you*?

A preamble to this issue would be to acknowledge that we are at the very threshold of the deepest of all mysteries in the universe, as Love, ultimately, is identified with God. However, we can assume that anyone who expresses love to the loved one in this way wishes to be a *single whole* with the beloved: such is the pull of him who is contemplated as the epitome of all beauty and the source of all imaginable goodness —which explains what the ancients said about love being a *uniting force*. Always keep in mind, however, that we are talking about *union of lives and not of persons*; the latter have to maintain at all times their peculiar and inalienable essential personalities, which is what allows the observation that in love *every one is each one*.

In merely human love, no matter how pure and lofty it may be, this *fusion of lives* is nothing more than a desire that does not go far beyond an identification of feelings, despite the biblical saying that *the two shall become one flesh* (Gen 2:24, Mt 19:5) and the comparison established by Saint Paul between conjugal love and the self–giving of

Christ to His Church (Eph 5:32). Legitimate conjugal love is indeed a true and lofty love, and it is one of the most sublime events that can happen to man during his earthly life. In fact, its *inferiority* as to its classification is based not on its nature but on its being compared with divine–human love or, even more so, with divine love. Therefore, the union by which the spouses become *one flesh* is reduced to a union that could be defined —according to a graduating scale and to the language that we have agreed to use in this particular case— as *secondary analogate love*.

Divine–human love —*primary analogate* in regard to pure Divine Love—, which effectively provides a *real* fusion of lives, is expressed in the Bible in utterances and idioms that necessarily have to be adapted to the limitations of human language: *He that eateth my flesh and drinketh my blood remains in me and I in him;*[17] the English version of *La Bible de Jérusalem* (Doubleday), for example, translates this as *lives in me and I live in that person...* or as Saint Paul also said, *I live; yet not I, but Christ liveth in me.*[18]

---

[17]Jn 6:56.

[18]Gal 2:20.

XV

...Do not say you love me then
For, were you ever to repeat that sweet sigh,
On hearing it, I may die.[1]

Since Sacred Scripture is akin to the Code of the love relationships between God and man, it is noteworthy that the expression *I love you* never appears there. That phrase is spoken only during one dialogue of Jesus with Saint Peter, and even then in a question–and–answer format, at the institution of the Primacy: *Do you love me?* or *Do you love me more than these?*[2] Saint Peter, in turn, answers in the affirmative; but only after he has uttered

---

[1] *CFC*, n. 52. In the Spanish original: ...no digas que me quieres,/ no muera yo al oírlo/ si acaso tú volvieras a decirlo.

[2] Jn 21:15.

—as if by way of mitigation and as if somehow being afraid regarding the content and profundity of the expression of openly confessing his feelings— these previous words: *Lord, you know it*, or *you know all things.*

Even the *Song of Songs*, filled with mutual compliments and wooing exchanges between the Bridegroom and the bride, does not contain the expression *I love you*. Both Bridegroom and bride openly declare to everybody the love they mutually profess and extol the many virtues and graces that each enthusiastically proclaims and recognizes as being possessed by the other; but at no time in the Holy Book does the assertion *I love you* or even any equivalent intimation appear.

But —one might ask—, why this reluctance to say it, and even more so when these books contain the Chronicles of such a perfect love as divine–human love? To answer this, it would be necessary to understand the most recondite mysteries of love and, which is still more difficult, be able to express them.

It should be noted that the aim of books is to narrate events, true or fictional, or to expound doctrines or the results of human speculation. But nobody can explain or communicate to others the mystery of true love.

The intimate *I love you* in divine–human love remains forever in the mysterious *one–to–one* correlation carried out between God and man. Saint Paul said that *Eye hath not seen, nor ear heard, neither have entered into the heart of man, the things that God hath prepared for them who love him*;[3] these words must not be referred only to Eternal Life, for there is no real reason to justify such a restriction of their meaning. It is easily forgotten that every true relationship of love —and above all of divine–human love— remains forever within the hidden and exclusive *thou and I* of both lovers; as the Apocalypse affirms: *He that hath an ear, let him hear what the Spirit saith unto the churches; To him that overcometh will I give to eat of the hidden manna, and will give him a white stone, and in the stone a new name written, which no man knoweth saving he that receiveth it.*[4]

Love has only one way of expressing itself which can match, and even surpass, uttering the phrase *I love you* and which lies at the opposite end of that expression in that it uses, as if by paradox, precisely *silence*. We are referring to the *silent gaze*, which is able to signify much deeper sentiments than words can convey.

The Gospel presents us with two distinct occasions on which this way of expressing love takes place. One has to

---

[3] 1 Cor 2:9.

[4] Rev 2:17.

do with the moment when Saint Peter, having denied his Master three times, meets Him and exchanges gazes with Him. Jesus, Who does not utter a word, communicates to His apostle with His eyes *all that can be said in silence by a heart that is overflowing with love more than ever before.* Saint Luke tells it in his recounting of the Passion: *And immediately, while he was still speaking, a cock crew. And the Lord turned and looked upon Peter. And Peter remembered the word of the Lord, how he had said unto him, 'Before the cock crows today, you will have disowned me three times.' And he went out and wept bitterly.*[5] In effect, were it not because of love, no one would ever have thought that silence could be even more expressive than words; especially since words in themselves are unable to contain the tremendous beauty and extraordinary grandeur intrinsic to feelings.

The other occasion in the Gospel has to do with the rich young man; the one who, having acknowledged before Jesus that he kept the commandments, heard from the lips of the Master that he was still lacking something: *And Jesus looked steadily at him and was filled with love for him, and he said...*[6] It is impossible to know just how much

---

[5]Lk 22: 60–62.

[6]Mk 10:21.

that gaze of Jesus revealed... and even more impossible to understand the mystery (inherent in human liberty) of how that young man could have hardened his heart enough to resist it.

The *Song of Songs*, as one would expect, also echoes this way of expressing love, speaking about that which words are unable to describe:

> *Thou hast ravished my heart, my sister, my spouse;*
> *Thou hast ravished my heart with a single one of*
> *   your glances,*
> *With a single link of your necklace.*[7]

Love holds a sacred moment in which even Nature wants to cooperate with its silence. For it is a fact that in the presence of the expression of true love, and none more so than divine–human love, the Universe can do nothing but remain silent:

> *Following shepherds and sheep,*
> *I came to where the Loved One awaited me*
> *Hidden in hillsides so deep;*
> *As he spoke to me softly*
> *The whistling sounds of the jungle ceased to be.*[8]

---

[7] Sg 4:9.

[8] *CFC*. n. 6. In the Spanish original: *Siguiendo a los pastores/ busqué donde el Amado me esperaba/ oculto en los alcores./ Y al tiempo que me hablaba/ el susurro del viento se escuchaba.*

For it was precisely during a silence, the deepest in all the History of the Universe, when the ineffable mystery of the Incarnation of the Son of God took place. That is how the sacred *Book of Wisdom* narrates it: *When a deep silence surrounded all things, and night had run the half of her swift course, down from the heavens, from the royal throne, leapt, O Lord, your all–powerful Word.*[9]

---

[9]Wis 18: 14–15.

XVI

The Master is here and calleth for thee...

With these words Martha told her sister Mary —informing her secretly— of the presence of the Master and His request that Mary come to meet Him.[1]

There is no other voice in the world that can fulfill the longings and yearnings of the heart as does the voice of God. It could very well be said that the ears and hearts of men were made especially to listen to, and even to be seduced exclusively by, that Voice.

As Jesus Christ Himself explained, the Good Shepherd *calleth his own sheep by name... and they follow him because they know his voice.*[2] His is a loving Voice that calls

---

[1] Jn 11:28.

[2] Jn 10: 3–4.

each of His sheep by name and they, in turn, recognize It. Since love is a personal *one–to–one* relationship of endearing intimacy (in reality, there is no relationship more intimate), it implies a deep and absolute intercourse and a mutual understanding between the two who love each other. Hence the testimony of the prophet Isaiah: *I am the Lord, who call thee by thy name,*[3] wherein the designation of the name of him whom God is calling indicates that it is an intimate and personal call, that is, a call of love. Therefore it also follows that any relationship which God establishes with man is necessarily a loving one within the framework of an intimacy which makes it clear that for Him every man is *a personal and unique being.*

On the other hand, since any *call,* by definition, always expects a *response,* it would clearly be a contradiction to assume, as the ideology of *Anonymous Christianity* does, that the offer of love by which God summons man to salvation is unilateral and that there is no need for the creature to accept it freely or even to know about it. According to the entire doctrine concerning love, to admit this unilateralism would be tantamount to squaring the circle.

Martha conveys to her sister Mary, precisely *in an aside,* that the Lord requested her to meet Him; for the

---

[3]Is 45:3.

relationship of love between two enamored persons —along with all its elements— does not desire publicity or want to be aired before others. Once more, a *one–to–one* relationship, personal intimacy, and a dear search for solitude appear together as something constantly sought by true lovers, for these are things which lovers have always procured:

> *Let's go to grassy meadows*
> *And await Dawn's rosy brightness in her stride,*
> *Forgotten by friends and foes;*
> *There in sweet peace we'll abide*
> *And hear the morning sounds of the countryside.*[4]

Unfortunately, the Catholic of the *New Church*, blessed by the *New Pentecost*, has lost sight of the transcendence of an intimate love relationship with a Personal God who is all Love. It could not have happened otherwise, for man has set himself up as the principal object of his own care, as if that were the most important thing, and no longer looks to the *Other* who is God; thus shattering any possibility of romance with Him.

---

[4]*CFC*, n. 106. In the Spanish original: *Vayamos a los prados,/ y a la rosada aurora esperaremos/ de todos olvidados./ Y allí nos quedaremos/ y el despertar del campo escucharemos.*

Therefore, man has submerged himself in the most horrific loneliness. For, if there is no *one–to–one* bond or intimacy between persons who give themselves to each other, then love becomes impossible; and so does any possibility of knowing God through the only path that can lead to Him, which is precisely love: *He that loveth not knoweth not God; for God is love.*[5] To make matters worse, there is a harsh corollary: he who is not able to talk to God and have a relationship with Him is absolutely incapable of carrying out any dialogue with other men except as a mere playing with words.

And as we have always noted, love can only be lived in its fullness and in its purest, most original condition within the divine–human relationship of love, even if we grant to purely human love the eminence which it truly deserves. It is in the former where love tends to reach the fullness of meaning. Indeed, the Voice of God is endowed with such clarity and such depth of expression that the human voice is reduced in comparison to an impoverished mode of communication, able to say only *something* of what it wants to express but can never convey. In divine–human love, however, metaphors and other figurative tropes or modes of expression are abandoned; here what is said is

---

[5] 1 Jn 4:8.

absolutely real and expresses the *full* content with which the heart is overflowing.

It is here that silence is extremely expressive, speaking without words but saying everything that it feels and everything that purely human language could never communicate:

> *There, at my Beloved's side,*
> *In the common land the wind murmuring words,*
> *Being I always at his side;*
> *In my ear he softly whispered*
> *That he too, wounded by my love, has suffered.*[6]
>
> *My Love, Stars in the Heavens,*
> *Seas kissed by bows of a thousand ships below,*
> *Eyes of sweet youthful maidens,*
> *Songs of wood thrush and sparrow,*
> *Everything I told you and which you now know...*[7]

But the Bridegroom's Voice is sometimes shifting and elusive, not easy to recognize and difficult to locate. Which

---

[6] *CFC*, n. 55. In the Spanish original: *Allí, junto al Amado/ mientras soplaba el cierzo en el ejido,/ a fuer de enamorado/ me susurró al oído/ que también por mi amor estaba herido.*

[7] *CFC*, n. 67. In the Spanish original: *Mi Amado, las estrellas,/ el mar que besan proas de mil naves,/ los ojos de doncellas,/ el canto de las aves,/ aquello que te dije y que tú sabes...*

is not hard to understand when one ponders, once again, what is generally known: the disciple of Jesus Christ is still a *traveler* who has not yet arrived at his Homeland. Like lovers who play the game of hide and seek, in a kind of *let me find you* whose only purpose is to increase the quality of a love which is already pure and authentic. It also is a recreation of love that the Bridegroom likes to engage in throughout the period of trial for the bride, in order to purify and increase the delicate affections which she assures to profess to Him:

> *The voice of my beloved! Behold, he cometh*
> *Leaping upon the mountains,*
> *Skipping upon the hills.*
> *My beloved is like a roe or a young hart,*
> *He standeth behind our wall,*
> *He looketh forth at the windows,*
> *He peers through the lattice.*[8]

In effect, this is the way the Bridegroom behaves during the period of testing which the bride must surpass: leaping upon the mountains and bounding over the hills like a gazelle or a young hart. He is evasive, elusive, inaccessible, difficult, unpredictable, and surprising.

---

[8]Sg 2: 8–9.

But one would be completely mistaken who attempts to see in His behavior toward the bride a purely practical or pedagogical intent. The truth is that, beyond all this, such comportment also has a *playful character*. For what is beyond doubt, although so far nobody has been able to explain it sufficiently, is that lovers enjoy playing in their intimate relationship; one more of the infinite aspects of the mysterious universe of love that still remain unknown: *the Spirit breatheth where he will and thou hearest his voice; but thou knowest not whence he cometh and whither he goeth.*[9] Could anybody perchance say where love comes from and how far it is able to take us...?

The peculiar thing about all this is that the bride, who perfectly understands the playful spirit that the Bridegroom wants to display in this relationship of love, is quite willing to support it, *although she would never be able to explain the reason for this mutual enjoyment*; ...and this is also part and parcel of any loving relationship. We have too often said that in love everything is reciprocal and equally shared. Therefore, if the Bridegroom plays, she also has fun; if the Bridegroom likes to be looked for, she also likes to hide; if the Bridegroom chooses to appear as if

---

[9] Jn 3:8.

He likes to be expected, she also takes pleasure in feigning
a delay... Therefore, the Bridegroom exclaims:

> *Beloved, I searched to see,*
> *In my orchard, the path where lemon blooms burst,*
> *There I stayed in wait for thee,*
> *Out behind my lemon tree,*
> *To see if, My Beloved, I found you first.*[10]

And the bride, in turn, answers:

> *My Love, I have walked anew*
> *On your orchard path where lemon blooms have burst.*
> *There I hid myself from you*
> *Behind lemon trees from view*
> *Just to see, My Love, if I could kiss you first.*[11]

---

[10] *CFC*, n. 46. In the Spanish original: *Amada, yo he buscado/ de
mi huerto de azahares el sendero,/ y luego te he esperado/ detrás del
limonero/ a ver si te encontraba yo primero.*

[11] *CFC*, n. 45. In the Spanish original: *Amado, he recorrido/ de tu
huerto de azahares el sendero,/ y luego me he escondido/ detrás del
limonero/ para poder besarte yo primero.*

XVII

At night he left for the distant mountain range,
At night he walked on the road around the bend,
At night I was left in foreign lands and strange,
At night I was found alone without my friend.[1]

Jesus ascended into Heaven before the astonished gaze of His Apostles and disciples who were totally entranced and paralyzed with the emotion of the moment. For a time they stood looking up, rapt in deep silence, overwhelmed with sadness, not knowing what to do or say. Then two angels shook them out of their reverie:

—*Men of Galilee, why stand you looking up to heaven?*[2]

---

[1] *CFC,* n. 23. In the Spanish original: *De noche se marchó hacia la montaña,/ de noche se perdió por el sendero,/ de noche me dejó por tierra extraña,/ de noche me encontré sin compañero.*

[2] Acts 1:11.

This reprimand was opportune; they were paralyzed because, for the first time in their lives, they were experiencing the brutal sense of true solitude. That instant was the most painful moment they could ever have envisaged: they were facing the reality of *being left without the Master.*

Establishing a parallelism, one could perhaps call to mind the moment when the Prophet Elijah was separated from his disciple Elisha —but without the despair suffered by Elisha and underlining the deep and passionate pain felt by the Apostles:

As they walked on, talking as they went, a chariot of fire appeared and horses of fire coming between the two of them; and Elijah went up to heaven in the whirlwind. Elisha saw it, and he shouted:

—My father! My father! Chariot of Israel and its chargers!

Then he lost sight of him, and taking hold of his own clothes he tore them in half.[3]

It is true that the Master had previously made them some momentous and consoling promises: *But I tell the truth: it is for your own good that I am going, because*

---

[3] 2 Kings 2: 11–12.

unless I go, the Paraclete will not come to you;[4] promises fully filled with hope: *I shall see you again, and your hearts will be filled with joy, and that joy no man shall take from you.*[5] However, everyone knows that words of consolation are only useful in helping to lift up one's heart and ease sadness; they can do no do more than that. Mitigating the pain caused by distressful feelings necessarily means, like it or not, that a remnant of sadness still lingers, becoming deep sorrow when it is rooted in great love.

The reality that Jesus Christ left them alone was something much more serious than they could ever have imagined at that moment, despite the magnitude of their pain. And Jesus Christ was well aware of it. That is why His Heart poured out a tremendously passionate, almost anguished, prayer addressed to His Father on the Night of His Farewell: *I am no longer in the world, but they are in the world, and I am coming to you*;[6] as if He had said: *Take this into account, Father: I am leaving, but they will have to stay...*

Centuries have passed since then, even millennia, and His disciples are still awaiting His Return. During this time, which is becoming such a long delay, many have

---

[4] Jn 16:7.

[5] Jn 16:22.

[6] Jn 17:11.

given up waiting and have even stopped believing in it: *Know this first, that there shall come in the last days scoffers, walking after their own lusts, and saying: What has happened to the promise of his coming? Since our Fathers died everything has gone on just as it has since the beginning of creation!*[7] Men, indeed, tend to behave in this way. That is why a moment finally arrives in which presence becomes merely remembrance; remembrance, vague memories; memories, legends; legends, myths; and myths... end up being lost in the mists of time, forever forgotten. It is then that watchful waiting begins to relax and is subsequently totally abandoned, as in the Parable of the Ten Virgins: *As the Bridegroom tarried, they all grew drowsy and fell asleep*;[8] although this is not the worst.

In effect, as time has gone by, the number of those who are still waiting for the Bridegroom has been in steady decline, while the crowds of *those who expect nothing* unceasingly increase. This situation led men to decide that it was here, and only here, where the *permanent city* should be built (Heb 13:14). Then the vast majority of people decided to stay in it because *there is nothing and no one to wait for.*

---

[7]2 Pet 3: 3–4.

[8]Mt 25:5.

Behold the terrible drama of the present time which men refuse to acknowledge: *A world without Hope is a desolate world* which has renounced forever Love and Joy and has made its option for a fearful abyss... at the bottom of which something far more terrible than Nothingness itself is sensed.

But there is still a *little flock* (Lk 12:32) that is longingly waiting for the return of their Shepherd. They are those who have always loved because, love being that mysterious thing that *never comes to an end* (1 Cor 13:8), they have never ceased waiting for His final Coming. The Apostle Saint Paul identifies love with nostalgia and longings for His coming: *All there is to come for me now is the crown of uprightness which the Lord, the upright judge, will give to me on that Day; and not only to me but to all those 'who have loved his coming.'*[9] He awaits nothing who loves nothing. Hence, it is clear once more that Hope always walks hand in hand with Love.

Encouraged by their hopeful Wait for the Bridegroom Who promised He would come back, Christians of all ages —especially present day Christians— have drawn strength to continue their journey in the midst of countless adversities. This Wait increases its sweet Nostalgia when it looks

---

[9] 2 Tim 4:8.

back on the past; and it burns with ardent longings for His quick return when it looks to the future:

The Spirit and the Bride say, 'Come!' Let him who listens answer, 'Come!'.

The one who attests these things says: Indeed I come soon. Amen; Come, Lord Jesus.[10]

Hope is the food of a love that suffers because of absences and nostalgia. Hope's role is not merely one of consolation; this virtue becomes an incentive to increase beyond one's thoughts the longings and desire to finally find the expected person, thus increasing love and intensifying the Perfect Joy of a final Meeting whose realization cannot be doubted.

This is precisely how the enamored soul felt when she, like the sensible Virgins of the Parable, was waiting with her lamp trimmed and lit:

> *In the peaceful calm of night*
> *Of the silent wooded valley without gloom,*
> *With soft sweet pain, now so right,*
> *The waiting for the Bridegroom*
> *Fills the soul with ardent, impatient delight.*[11]

---

[10]Rev 22: 17.20.

[11]*CFC*, n. 108. In the Spanish original: *En la noche serena/ del silencioso valle nemoroso,/ en honda y dulce pena,/ la espera del Esposo/ de ardorosa impaciencia mi alma llena.*

XVIII

Come, my dearest love, come to my side at last,
My Spouse, my perfect one, my dove so serene,
For already the night runs, hurrying fast,
And behind the hill the sun can now be seen.[1]

In the mysterious world of divine–human love not yet consummated in the Homeland, this exclamation of the Bridegroom regarding the end of night and the nearness of day is a cry of Hope. Saint Paul expressed it in one concise sentence: *The night is far spent, the day is at hand.*[2] In effect, the texts of the Scripture refer to the culmination of the earthly pilgrimage and its resulting End.

---

[1] *CFC.* n. 81. In the Spanish original: *Ven por fin a mi lado, bien-amada,/ mi esposa, mi perfecta, mi paloma,/ pues ya la noche corre apresurada/ y el sol por el otero ya se asoma.*

[2] Rom 13:12.

But there are many in the society of men who think that Death is the ultimate termination. Among them are those for whom this life offers the only happiness to which man can aspire (even though they realize that it is a diminished happiness); others, however, consider human existence as something Absurd where beings destined for Nothingness are writhing.

Things are quite different for Christians. As the Apostle also says: *We are not of the night, nor of the darkness.*[3] Consequently, Life presents them with a double meaning:

First, as the fullness of Joy, in that Life, besides being the Road that leads definitively to their Homeland provides them with the opportunity to share the existence and Death of Jesus Christ.

Second, Life, seen from another point of view, is for them a true *Valley of Tears* in which they cover a journey that is identified with the steep, narrow, and difficult path announced by the Master (Mt 7:14). Christians traverse it accompanied by suffering and pain in all its forms —as well as incomprehension and persecution from a World that will never forgive them their status as disciples of Jesus Christ.

---

[3] 1 Thess 5:5.

Throughout this journey, Christians, logically, are yearning, earnestly desiring that the darkness, night, winter, and rain may cease. At the same time, they live encouraged by a variety of feelings of nostalgia, aspirations, thrills —in brief, on Hope; with the consolation of knowing that this period of trials and pilgrimage is short, for they have already been told that *time is short*[4] and that *the appearance of this world passeth away*.[5]

The Bridegroom of the *Song of Songs* is much more impatient than the bride for the time of their meeting to arrive. The absence of one of the lovers is hard to bear by the other; only Hope, which provides the certainty that this situation is temporary, endows the lovers with the strength they need to keep waiting for the moment when they may see each other again. That is why the Bridegroom, elated, encourages her:

> *The voice of my beloved!...*
> *My beloved spoke, and said unto me,*
> *Rise up, my love,*
> *My fair one, and come away.*
> *For, lo, the winter is past,*
> *The rain is over and gone.*[6]

---

[4] 1 Cor 7:29.

[5] 1 Cor 7:31.

[6] Sg 2: 8.10–11.

And, as in love everything is equality and reciprocity, it is the bride, now as impatient as the Bridegroom, who calls Him persistently so that He will soon come and set her free from the danger of succumbing to the coldness of the air and the darkness of the night:

> *Before the day–breeze rises,*
> *And the shadows flee away,*
> *Return, my beloved, and be thou like a roe*
> *Or a young hart upon the mountains of Bether.*[7]

The longing that moves Christians to live on Hope is as strong as the feelings caused in them by the suffering they are forced to undergo —to which it must be added the feeling of being strangers, which they necessarily must endure because they are surrounded by the hostile environment of the World in which they live. These hostilities and consequent feelings are now stronger and more acute than ever before because today's Christians now seem to lack even the secure shelter accorded yesteryear by the Church; she who is now suffering a crisis of insecurity about Herself which is aggravated, in turn, by the way many bad Shepherds behave.

---

[7]Sg 2:17.

However, the major and most important source of suffering which often goes unnoticed by many of them, is the lukewarmness which affects Christian life in general: *The only sadness is not to be a saint.* Love does not at all get along with mediocrity, since love is essentially *totality* and does not understand any kind of partiality, conditions, or delays; it gives everything now and hopes also to receive fully and immediately. Hence the timeliness of the Master's words: *For unto every one that hath shall be given, and he shall have abundance: but from him that hath not shall be taken away even that few things which he hath.*[8]

True lovers, however, live longingly awaiting the end of the night and the coming of the day. They glimpse, at last, the disappearance of the shadows and begin to sense, in a strange but true manner, the clear sounds of melodious strains that overwhelm the soul, liberate it from the World, and, at the same time, make it perceive the harmonies of Heaven:

---

[8] Mt 25:29.

The lights that morning was already pouring
brought back joyful life to the deep green valley;
And one could hear, at times, in the far ravine
Strumming that combines soft rhythmic melody
Like quaint guitars and rebecs
And droning murmurs of cicada insects.[9]

---

[9] *CFC*, n. 31. In the Spanish original: *Los rayos que la aurora derramaba/ la vida al verde valle devolvían,/ mientras que en las cañadas se escuchaba/ el melodioso son, que al par hacían,/ rabeles y guitarras/ y el áspero runrún de las cigarras.*

XIX

Who against all hope believed in hope...[1]

This text of Saint Paul undoubtedly is one of the cornerstones of Christian life. Everything seems to indicate that the meaning of this phrase is that Christian Hope begins when all hope based on merely human grounds is gone. Or, put another way, this passage bears witness to the fact that the virtue of Hope does not fully burst into the life of a Christian *until every single trace of human hope has ceased to exist.*

Indeed, to affirm that Christian Hope is the only one that does not disappoint (Rom 5:5) means that *all human hopes are fallacious*; although, oddly enough, they

---

[1] Rom 4:18.

nowadays enjoy public acceptance and credibility as never before. Never before has Humanity felt such an intense desire to be deceived as it does now.

It is a known fact that purely human hopes enjoy universal acceptance; even more, negating them merely brings about the enmity of the World —and even persecution of those who dare to question them; despite the fact that they are based upon monstrous lies and imaginary *utopias*.

And the utopias on which modern society lives and feeds are nothing more than cunning deceits, crafted and fostered by the Spirit of Evil in order to keep modern man trapped in a dangerous illusion. The malice of utopias is that they make their followers live in a *continuous lie* that both separates them from reality and compels them to forget the object of their real hope, encouraging them to follow a path that leads to their inevitable perdition. Utopias, by simply keeping men in a constant state of delusion and falsehood, are beneficial for the Father of all Lies; after all, this state of deception is the most impenetrable opposition imaginable to Him Who said that He was the Truth (Jn 14:6).

The Utopia of Justice

There are still some who think that a time will come when someone —a particular system, a political party, or maybe some adept government or president— will finally establish Justice in the world. It is a vain hope, *which no one really believes*, regardless of how abundantly men speak about justice, its independence, and the separation of Powers within the public square; which, incidentally, is a doctrine that *has not been achieved anywhere*, no matter how much some people continue to maintain the opposite opinion.

The Bible, for example, does not believe that true Justice will ever be established in the world during the present Time. Saint Peter said that *we look for new heavens and a new earth according to his promises, in which justice dwelleth.*[2] From this it follows that if justice will reign only when this momentous time in the History of Salvation is reached, it is because such a thing will never come to pass in the world of the Pilgrim Church.

Moreover, contrary to what ordinarily would be logical to think, *Humanity does not really have any desire for justice.* In this world the number of unjust people and those who live outside honesty are legion, and they do

---

[2] 2 Pet 3:13.

not have the slightest desire to change things. So it may very well be said that the society of men is the Kingdom of Injustice, as anyone can verify without demonstration just by looking around himself. As for biblical arguments on this point (for a Christian, the Word of God is the ultimate criterion of knowledge), it should be noted that Jesus Christ Himself called them blessed *who hunger and thirst for justice*. And the term *blessed* always refers to a minority, also according to words of Christ Himself, Who said that those who walk upon the Road that leads to life are very few while, conversely, many are on the Road to perdition (Mt 7: 13–14).

From this it follows that, once Democracy has been raised to the category of an article of faith, the constant chatter of modern society about justice is reduced, ultimately, to a gigantic exercise in collective self–deception and hypocrisy. The now old and inveterate agreement with the Lie has led Humanity to give worship to the Father of all Falsehoods and all liars.

Hence the Christian cannot believe in utopias, for he cannot accept the Lie nor agree with it. He does believe in Justice, in every one of its various forms, as the individual virtue that is to govern his personal life; and also as Hope of something loftier but which will only become reality in the World to come. Thus, Justice is for him a *future reality* in which he now trusts by the virtue of Hope, which gives him strength to look forward and liberates him from believing in an alleged current reality which is nothing but pure falsehood because *it is not seen or found anywhere.* This is how, thanks to Hope, the Christian lives rooted in truth and is nourished by that nostalgia and longings that will never let him down: *For we are saved by hope. But hope that is seen, is not hope. For what a man seeth, why doth he hope for? But if we hope for that which we see not, we wait for it with patience.*[3]

Lastly, the disciple of Jesus Christ is well aware that he will never find Justice for the duration of his earthly pilgrimage. And even less Peace, which has always been a sister to Justice and is never without It (Ps 85:11) until the radiant glow of the morning star illuminates the new day (2 Pet 1:19). It will be then that the Bridegroom will arrive and will make real what was heralded by the Apocalypse, once all hope has been accomplished: *God shall wipe away all tears from their eyes; and death shall be no more, nor mourning, nor crying, nor sorrow shall be any more, for the former things are passed away* (Rev 21:4). So the verse also says:

---

[3]Rom 8: 24–25.

Blessed is he who has ardently loved
Find traces of the friend beloved and true
And at last he reached and embraced at road's end
What he had known only in Hope before then.[4]

---

[4] *CFC*, n. 117. In the Spanish original: *Dichoso aquél que ardiente ha deseado/ hallar las huellas del amigo amado/ hasta que, ya cansado, al fin alcanza/ lo conocido antaño en esperanza.*

XX

Without concern they dress my people's wound, saying, "Peace! Peace!" whereas there is no peace.[1]

As we have said, the evil of utopias is that they take man away from real hopes, making him conceive false dreams which take him away from his end and lead him to perdition. For the Spirit of Evil tries by all means to separate man from the truth and steer him towards the lie by striving to fill his heart with vain utopias and futile dreams that can make him forget the deep content of Christian Hope. Actually, not many people come to understand the reality expressed by Fernández de Andrada:

---

[1] Jer 6:14.

> *Fabio, courtesans hopes*
> *Prisons are where the ambitious dies*
> *And where the cleverest grows grey hair.*
> *He who does not file them off or break them,*
> *Has not earned the name of man,*
> *Nor access to the honor he has sought.*[2]

And it is a tremendous misfortune for any man to have lost the virtue of Hope. He who has not come to know Christian Hope, or has decided to ignore It, has sentenced himself to spend his life without joy or expectations, aimlessly walking around like a blind man whose fate cannot be other than the abyss. The permanent loss of Christian Hope is tantamount to the *eternal loss of love*, and, therefore, to the absolute forfeiture of the end for which man has been created. Dante expressed this reality in the inscription on the frontispiece of the gate of the Inferno of his *Divine Comedy*:

> *Through me the way is to the city dolent;*
> *Through me the way is to eternal dole;*
> *Through me the way among the people lost.*
> *Justice incited my sublime Creator;*
> *Created me divine Omnipotence,*

---

[2]Fernández de Andrada, *Moral Letter to Fabius.*

> *The highest Wisdom and the primal Love.*
> *Before me there were no created things,*
> *Only eterne, and I eternal last.*
> *All hope abandon, ye who enter in!*

Therefore, this, and no other, is the end of all the false hopes and utopias. Let us see briefly, by way of example, some of the most common utopias in today's world.

The Utopia of Peace

The Utopia of pacifism is one of the greatest hoaxes in which modern society lives voluntarily. Never before has there been so much talk about peace; everybody has proclaimed it, but *in fact, nobody does anything to procure it.* It is not easy to accurately determine the objectives of *pacifism*, but they could be summarized, ultimately, as the same as the aims of *feminism.* Both agree in their attempt to dissolve modern society as it is structured according to the Christian foundations still extant in it. Some also speak of a strategy to dominate weak nations by the most powerful; others prefer to think of the vain belief in establishing universal Peace overseen by a World Government that would extend over the entire planet and end war forever. These apparently diverse ends share a common purpose: to utterly destroy the last Christian roots still present in modern society.

However, Peace as the absence of war —which is how the World understands it— is but an illusion and a utopia. In short, an impossibility in which only the naive or those who have been seduced by the Lie can believe; for they have turned their minds from the truth to make way for fables, as the Apostle Saint Paul says (2 Tim 4:4). It would be wonderful, indeed, to be able to believe in this universal Peace; yet, it is much better to side with truth, however unpleasant it may seem. Utopia is, after all, a false dream and a lie; therefore, to accept it is to walk on the path to perdition.

Of course, the New Testament, besides ignoring the concept of peace as the World understands it, rejects the idea that the so–insistently touted universal Peace can ever be achieved, even making fun of such a monster–size concoction: *For when they shall say, Peace and safety; then sudden destruction cometh upon them, as travail upon a woman with child; and they shall not escape.*[3]

Jesus Christ Himself, speaking of the events leading up to the end of History, does not seem to agree with the idea that men will obtain some day this happy, global

---

[3] 1 Thess 5:3

Peace. He rather announces the opposite: *And when ye shall hear of wars and rumours of wars, be ye not troubled: for such things must needs be; but the end shall not be yet. For nation shall rise against nation, and kingdom against kingdom: and there shall be earthquakes in divers places, and there shall be famines and troubles: these are the beginnings of sorrows.*[4] There cannot be Peace without Justice; and since the World is so far from giving the latter a chance —and one cannot see the slightest hint of change to the contrary—, only those who have made their final choice for the Lie could believe in this dreamt–of universal Peace. It is indeed demonstrated that all liars convince themselves of their own fallacies, and finally become victims of them.

The saddest part of this problem is that even Christians themselves have forgotten the true meaning of Peace, as Jesus Christ understood it. The Church herself, which has spoken of and still speaks about Peace through a constant Pastoral activity, seems to know no peace other than worldly Peace. Therefore, the worst thing that could happen to a present day Christian is not the feeling of being immersed in a sea of confusion, *but the fact of having lost Joy.* A misfortune that is possible only when one loses

---

[4]Mk 13: 7–8.

sight of the concept of Peace as Jesus Christ bequeathed It to His own: *Peace I leave with you, my peace I give unto you: not as the world giveth, give I unto you.*[5] That is why the Apostle said: *And the peace of God, which passeth all understanding, shall keep your hearts and minds through Christ Jesus.*[6]

Jesus Christ carefully distinguished His Peace from the one that the World gives. Also, and contrary to the way followed by false ideologies, He *does not promise* His disciples a future Peace, He *already grants it, at this moment.* So their hopes are mixed with accompanying feelings of Joy: *And ye now therefore have sorrow: but I will see you again, and your heart shall rejoice, and your joy no man taketh from you.*[7] This is a promise that has nothing to do with utopia, since it, unlike utopia, is not based on the Lie, but on Him who said of Himself *I am the Truth.*[8]

---

[5]Jn 14:27.

[6]Phil 4:7.

[7]Jn 16:22.

[8]Jn 14:6.

XXI

Therefore my heart is glad,
And my soul rejoiceth;
My flesh also shall rest in hope.[1]

As we have frequently said, those who make their way through this Valley of Tears on their pilgrimage toward Heaven their Homeland are finding that the journey is becoming increasingly more excruciating and difficult; until they learn how to uncover the purpose of the afflictions that transform their journey into the arduous, steep, and difficult path of which the Gospel speaks (Mt 7:14); subsequently, those afflictions now acquire now a new significance.

---

[1] Ps 16:9.

These afflictions and hardships are very real, for the World is visibly crumbling. The Church, for example, whose number of faithful is diminishing progressively, has become increasingly confused, even to the danger of disappearing in the estimation of anyone who thinks profoundly about her and may have forgotten or never known the Promise of her Founder. The family as the foundation and stabilizing fabric of Society has every appearance of being doomed to a rapid dissipation. Freedoms exist only in name, for the State has established itself as a mammoth Monster controlling even the most intimate aspects of its citizens' lives. The Father of all Falsehoods, who has been acknowledged as Lord of the World (Jn 12:31; 16:11), has everywhere established his Kingdom of Lies and Injustice and has managed to subvert and make void the whole scale of human values as they have hitherto been understood. Christianity is being persecuted in either a bloody or bloodless way everywhere. Reason has disappeared — to the point that admitting the possibility of any certainty has become almost a crime. Love has been degraded to mere sex and equated with the most heinous aberrations. Human existence has ceased to make sense, since man believes it to be irrefutable that he is not the master of his own destiny, which also ends definitively with death.

Now more than ever it can be said that the way of any human being, especially that of the Christian who walks it as a pilgrim, passes through a Valley of Tears filled with severe suffering and sorrows.

However, man was not created for sorrow but rather for living in Bliss and reveling in Joy, which he has already begun during his earthly pilgrimage and which will be permanently realized in his Heavenly Homeland.

The problem is that the fundamentals that comprise the pillars of human existence are easily forgotten and are often even unknown. Suffering, for example, whose immense value and infinite potentialities, once it is properly understood, is usually held in contempt. However, suffering, when it is caused by love and once it has been sanctified by grace, is the *only chance that the Christian has to achieve Perfect Joy.*

That is how what are normally regarded as punishment and disgrace —suffering, pain, and death...— become, instead, the way of sharing the existence of Jesus Christ and of becoming part of the divine–human love relationship. Hence the necessity and grandeur of tribulations: *We glory also in tribulations, knowing that tribulation worketh patience; and patience tested character; and tested char-*

acter hope; and hope confoundeth not: because the charity of God is poured forth in our hearts...[2]

That is the reason for Hope; and this is how Love, although It is not wholly possessed yet (now only as a pledge and first fruits), is assured to be attained, thus filling the Christian pilgrim in this World with Joy despite the adversities of the hostile environment in which he lives. For the Apostle Saint Paul, Hope, and only Hope, could make him joyful in the midst of tribulation; thus, he said that the disciples of Jesus Christ should be at all times *rejoicing in hope, patient in tribulation, constant in prayer;*[3] a precept which has been forgotten by or remains unknown to a large number of Christians.

The theme of Love not yet entirely owned, which leads to the longing sighs brought by Hope and proper to the soul in love with God, deserves a special consideration. For, is it possible that the absence of the greatly desired Bridegroom (despite the certainty that He will be found soon) could feed the fiery yearnings of a soul in love with God? Can a painful absence be transformed into an unquenchable source of ineffable Joy? As Saint John of the Cross said in his *Spiritual Canticle*:

---

[2]Rom 5: 3–5.
[3]Rom 12:12.

Oh who my grief can mend!
Come, make the last surrender that I yearn for,
And let there be an end
Of messengers you send
Who bring me other tidings than I burn for.

Or, as the rhyme also expresses:

In the peaceful calm of night
Of the silent, wooded valley without gloom,
With deep sorrow, now so right,
The waiting for the Bridegroom
Fills the soul with longing, impatient delight.[4]

---

[4] *CFC*, n. 108. In the Spanish original: *En la noche serena/ del silencioso valle nemoroso,/ en honda y dulce pena,/ la espera del Esposo/ de ardorosa impaciencia mi alma llena.*

XXII

Hope and fullness of love.

Hope is the virtue that alleviates the hardships of the pilgrim Christian as he makes his way through the Valley of Tears; at the same time, It gives him strength to carry on until he reaches Home.

As the difficulties that besiege such an arduous journey increase, the need for Hope becomes more evident. A time comes in which It appears to be exhausted and even turned into despair —to the point that It seems to have disappeared leaving no trace. It is precisely then that the urgency of Hope's presence becomes more acutely felt, as the *hoping against hope* of Saint Paul suggests.[1] Therefore, it may very well be said that Hope does not fully

---

[1]Rom 4:18.

enter into action until the exact moment of Its apparent absence.

In the last analysis, Hope is what assures Christians that the colossal apparatus of this World, with the full force of Its Power, is but a passing breeze that leaves no trace: *For the fashion of this world passes away.*[2]

But Hope is not merely a consoling virtue; *It is the true source of Christian Joy.* For, as we have said, Hope provides the Christian with the confidence to wait with full certainty for the consoling reality that, in the end, an all–embracing Justice will dawn in the World of Lies and Injustice: *For we through the Spirit wait for the hope of righteousness by faith.*[3]

Love, that participation in Divine Life which is offered to every human being, does not become perfect while his earthly pilgrimage lasts. It is true that the presence of the Spirit in him is a reality (Rom 5:5), but only as first fruits (Rom 8:23); therefore this love is not yet a full possession. We have been saved, indeed, but as a possibility that is only hope for now (Rom 8:24).

For in the current Plan of the History of Salvation, the creature, fallen because of sin but regenerated by grace, reaches the fullness of love *step by step* walking the as-

---

[2]1 Cor 7:31.

[3]Gal 5:5.

cending path to perfection. His present state is, therefore, an *already* which is made up mainly of *not yet*. Nevertheless, this partial possession in regard to totality in love, far from being a cause for despondency, becomes *an inexhaustible source of joy that remains for the duration of the pilgrimage.*

First, because this living in the state of the *not yet* compels the creature to prepare gradually for total love, placing her in a situation in which she feeds on longings, impatience, anticipation of what is to come, expectation for the coming of the Bridegroom, and on a burning thirst to behold and enjoy His presence, as Saint John of the Cross said in his *Spiritual Canticle*:

> *Reveal your presence clearly*
> *And kill me with the beauty you discover,*
> *For pains acquired so dearly*
> *From love, cannot recover*
> *Save only through the presence of the lover.*

It is noteworthy here that such longing, far from turning into feelings of dejection and despair, fills the heart of the creature with joy. The Poet Saint of Fontiveros admits in this stanza that the hoped–for contemplation of the Bridegroom —actually, the mere possibility that such a thing might occur— can lead to his death by love. This same sentiment is experienced by the bride of the *Song of Songs*:

> *Stay me with raisin cakes,*
> *Comfort me with apples:*
> *For I languish with love.*[4]

This is precisely what makes the bride eagerly await the coming of the Bridegroom, for she cannot live without seeing Him or contemplating Him. She has finally realized that love is the only source of life that exists in the Universe; hence she considers unheard–of the situation of so many men who have not understood this and whose existence is nothing, therefore, but a pure shadowing of what true life would be:

> *I traveled the hills to be*
> *Where the springs of sweet and living waters rise,*
> *Awaiting my Love to see*
> *If at last he'd come to me*
> *And reveal to me the brightness of his eyes.*[5]

---

[4]Sg 2:5.

[5]In the Spanish original: *Anduve hasta el collado,/ donde mana la fuente de agua clara,/ a espera del Amado/ hasta que al fin llegara/ y el brillo de sus ojos me mostrara.*

This is why contemplating the Bridegroom at last and dying out of love are for her one and the same thing:

> *If only in my walking through the valley*
> *By the fir tree forest I could meet with you,*
> *And could contemplate you finally anew,*
> *Death from love I would share with you completely!ci*[6]

It should be noted that we are here at the exact opposite of the theory of *anonymous Christianity*, according to which salvation occurs automatically, without any acceptance or cooperation from man who would be living in a phantasmagoric, so called divine–human love relationship; for in this theory, a real divine–human love relationship is utterly destroyed.

Contrary to what common knowledge about love might suggest, the impatience and longing for the loved one, whose arrival and appearance are expected, are already in themselves enough to fill the heart with Joy. It should be noted that love is the most mysterious reality there is; hence it is no wonder that even the language of lovers is

---

[6] *CFC*, n. 27. In the Spanish original: *¡Si al recorrer el valle yo pudiera/ en el bosque de abetos encontrarte,/ hasta que al fin de nuevo al contemplarte/ muerte de amor contigo compartiera...!*

so unique and singular that only the two lovers can understand it. It is not uncommon, for example, that its content sometimes can express the opposite of what it apparently tries to say. As it happens in the following stanza, where what the beloved is really being asked is exactly the opposite of what a superficial spectator might believe:

> *If you should see me again,*
> *Down in the glen where the singing blackbirds fly,*
> *Do not say you love me then*
> *For, were you ever to repeat that sweet sigh,*
> *On hearing it, I may die.*[7]

Meanwhile, during the interval and the expectation, whether the enamored soul hears *I love you* again or not, she is pierced by and drowning in joy.

Anything that happens in the mysterious Universe of love is incomprehensible to someone who has never known how to love. Tears, for example, which are generally considered by everyone as an expression of sorrow, are, in love, one of the greatest expressions of joy that any human being can ever imagine; the spiritual writers refer to

---

[7] *CFC*, n. 52. In the Spanish original: *Si de nuevo me vieres,/ allá en el valle, donde canta el mirlo,/ no digas que me quieres,/ no muera yo al oírlo/ si acaso tú volvieras a decirlo.*

them as *the gift of tears.* For, as Gandalf, the character in Tolkien's epic work, said, *not all tears are an evil.* The tears shed by the appropriately named *weeping willow* who sees the sweet and enamored nightingale who has not yet found her beloved, are tears of compassion in love. And to suffer out of love, along with him who dies of love, is also experiencing the joy of love:

> *Sweet Philomena again*
> *Calls to her love from among the highest leaves*
> *Of a green willow tree in the shaded ford.*
> *And the tree shares the great pain*
> *Of the bird who seeks her love with no reward;*
> *Who in lonely sorrow grieves*
> *And feels in herself the sweet flames of love blaze*
> *And, from that hour, whenever*
> *He hears her grieving, the willow weeps for her.*[8]

---

[8] *CFC.* n. 16. In the Spanish original: *La dulce filomena/ llamando está a su amor desde la rama/ del verde sauce en el umbroso vado./ Y el árbol siente pena/ por el ave que no encuentra a su amado/ y que, en su angustia, clama,/ sintiendo que agoniza en dulce llama./ Y, desde aquella hora,/ siempre que la oye el sauce, también llora.*

XXIII

*I am filled with comfort, I am exceedingly joyful
In all our tribulations.*[1]

Another reason why the Christian is filled with joy because of Hope is that he has been given the opportunity to *share the sufferings and death of Jesus Christ.* But first he must know and love Jesus Christ; therefore, not many are able to truly live this mystery of Faith.

Chesterton said that *joy is the gigantic secret of the Christian.* This happy idea of the English writer has been embraced by the world as an ingenious literary phrase... though into whose meaning almost no one dares to delve; indeed, does anyone really believe that there are many

---

[1] 2 Cor 7:4.

Christians living their faith as a testimony of overflowing Joy? At best, there are some good Christians who are still willing to admit that trials and sufferings, when borne with patience, significantly contribute to easing their way to Heaven. But there is a great distance —and only a few cover it— between that approach and actually loving sufferings, lusting after them and receiving them with joy whereby one shares more fully the existence of Jesus Christ. Indeed, even if one accepts as true the statement of Chesterton, it should be acknowledged, nevertheless, that Joy is still a secret... even for Christians.

Yet this is precisely —at least it should be —*the natural condition of Christian life.* As the Apostle Paul clearly warned the Christians at Thessalonica: *No man should be moved in these tribulations, for yourselves know that we are appointed thereunto* (1 Thess 3:3). And if there were any doubt, we have his triumphant testimony in favor of the faithful at Macedonia, as it is mentioned in his Second Letter to the Corinthians: *How that in a great trial of affliction the abundance of their joy and their deep poverty abounded unto the riches of their liberality.*[2]

If this has always been difficult to understand for the large mass of Christians superficially living their Faith —not to mention purely carnal men who are unable to

---

[2] 2 Cor 8:2.

understand the things of the Spirit (1 Cor 2:14)—, what could be said of modern Catholicism, *updated as it has become to the mindset of the modern world*, which has substituted the worship of man for the worship of God, thus giving rise to a religion in which all notion of sacrifice and personal immolation out of love has been banished? The result, too patent to the eyes of anybody who wants to see, is a contemporary Catholicism, in harmony with the World in which it lives, which *has eliminated any vestige of Joy from the horizon of its existence.*

The serious issue posed by Christian existence, intelligible only to the true disciple of Jesus Christ, focuses on sharing His sufferings and His death (Rom 6:3). But we are not talking only about the Joy of sharing the life of the Master in each and every one of its facets —including its hardships and anxieties—, but about something much deeper and complex: indeed, which true lover does not wish to be with his beloved, and more so during hard times, and to even give his own life for her if that were possible? And yet, as stated above, this view and the assessment of this issue given so far must be surpassed —notwithstanding the fact that the Catholicism more attuned to the Universal Religion of the New Age seems to have forgotten it; for here we contemplate the joyful reality that *Jesus Christ is the very life of the Christian; he can no longer manage without Him throughout his earthly pilgrimage.* The great pioneer of Christian existence, the Apostle Saint Paul, expressed it beautifully when he said that *to me to live is Christ, and to die is gain.*[3]

Religious Poetry has tried to express, at least to the extent that human language and forms of expression allow it, just how impossible it is for the soul in love to live without Jesus Christ, both in joy and in pain, which, in turn, also become joy when experienced with Him and in Him:

> *His loving eyes looked at me*
> *Before the morning sun appeared in the sky,*
> *And they wounded me gravely*
> *With such sweet love that if I*
> *Could not see them again, I would surely die.*[4]

At other times, the soul tries to describe the exultation of finding the Master, at long last, by likening it to the happy transition from winter to spring. Meanwhile, the soul continues in relentless search of Him, suffering with sorrow when she thinks that He does not answer nor hear

---

[3] Phil 1:21.

[4] *CFC*, n. 33. In the Spanish original: *Sus ojos me miraron/ antes que el claro sol apareciera,/ y herido me dejaron/ de amor, en tal manera,/ que sin verlos de nuevo pereciera.*

her sore complaints. Until finally the soul finds peace in imagining that she is at His side, while listening, at a distance, to the sorrowful singing of birds, which is but a metaphorical reference to the noise of the world.

So far, this is a possible *explanation*, wrapped and hidden in metaphors, of the three stanzas that follow and form a unity; *possible explanation* because, as is well known, poetic language comes alive and speaks on its own, suggesting very different ideas to each individual listener. This is, again, the mysterious magic of Poetry: it becomes independent even of its author, a sort of orphan with unknown father or mother. This, and nothing else, is the grandeur and beauty of Poetry. One can say, indeed, that language is a *living thing*; but this is never truer than when applied to Poetry.

> *Since winter has finished its cycle and passed,*
> *Spring displays the first colourful flowers at last*
> *And now the woods are filled with fragrance and trills*
> *And the sweet lark takes wing high above the hills.*
>
> *In search of your footprints, I follow the trail*
> *Which rises uphill from the long and deep vale*
> *And suffering in anguish when you hide*
> *And to my sad complaints you have not replied.*

And in the soft mellowing evenings of spring
As if once more by your side I were lying
In the warm shade of the forest of larch trees
I hear the sweet lark in her sorrow she grieves.[5]

And at other times, the enamored soul has manifested these same feelings in a more simple and naïve but extremely heartfelt manner:

I looked but found you nowhere,
I called you with no reply;
When at last I saw you there,
I fainted with loving sigh.

I have lived in darkness bleak
Feeding on nostalgia's pain,
From lovesickness, wounded weak,
I die since I searched in vain.

---

[5] *CFC*, n. 28. In the Spanish original: *Ya el gélido invierno su ciclo fenece,/ y la primavera sus flores ofrece,/ ya el bosque se llena de trinos y aromas/ y vuela la alondra del valle a las lomas.// En pos de tus huellas fui por el sendero/ que del hondo valle sube hasta el otero,/ sufriendo de angustias porque al fin te fuiste/ y a mis tristes quejas no me respondiste.// Y en las suaves tardes de la primavera,/ como si a tu lado de nuevo estuviera,/ al pie del alerce y a su tibia sombra,/ el lamento escucho de la triste alondra.*

Have you heard my moans and tears...?
Has my sorrow, as I grieve,
Borne on wings of winds that breathe,
Come to you or reached your ears...?[6]

The World constantly speaks about a Peace that has actually disappeared from the horizon and its ends. As for Joy... the new Catholicism, so much preferred by modern man and whose precepts are nowadays so easily kept by *everybody*, has lost sight of its old Heroes: those men and women who accomplished exploits almost mythical and verging on the legendary; those whom former Christians admired and knew as Saints...; this neo–modernist Catholicism has degraded Love to a mere transient *solidarity* or has utterly forgotten It. The adherents of the *New Church*, brought about by the *New Pentecost* at the start of the present millennium, has forgotten the Joy of sharing the Cross and the bliss of personal immolation for the sake of the Beloved; at the same time, they feel

---

[6] *CFC*, n. 29. In the Spanish original: *Te busqué, mas no te hallé,/ te llamé, mas no te oí,/ y cuando, al fin, te encontré,/ por tu amor desfallecí.// En la oscuridad he vivido/ de nostalgia alimentado,/ y tan de amores herido/ que muero pues no te he hallado.// ¿Oíste al fin mis gemidos...?/ ¿Por fin mi triste lamento,/ llevado en alas del viento,/ ha llegado a tus oídos...?*

ashamed of the Church's glories of over twenty centuries and try to bury them, while betraying the set of sublime values led by virginity and holiness...

The fact is that peace, true peace, and Perfect Joy, sung by the Saint of Assisi, can only be found in the company and in the presence of Jesus Christ. As religious Poetry also recounted:

> *And there my ended woes and sorrows left me*
> *There where our lives are joined as one, by the sea*
> *Rocked with gentle waves created easily*
> *By the stirred blue waters lapping lazily.*[7]

---

[7] *CFC*, n. 105. In the Spanish original: *Y allí fueron mis penas fenecidas/ junto al mar que vio unidas nuestras vidas,/ mecido en suaves ondas, producidas/ por las azules aguas removidas.*

XXIV

My Love, Stars in the Heavens,
Seas kissed by bows of a thousand ships below,
Eyes of sweet youthful maidens,
Songs of wood thrush and sparrow,
Everything I told you and which you now know.[1]

Every love relationship *begins* with a dialogue between persons; except in the bosom of the Divine Trinity, where there are no starting, continuing, or ending moments. Thus it is said that the Son, the Word of the Father, is begotten in a *today* that is an instantaneous eternal present which

---

[1] *CFC*, n. 67. In the Spanish original: *Mi amado, las estrellas,/ el mar que besan proas de mil naves,/ los ojos de doncellas,/ el canto de las aves,/ aquello que te dije y que tú sabes.*

lacks beginning, duration, and end: *The Lord hath said to me; Thou art my son, this day have I begotten thee.*[2]

Of course, the same thing does not happen with human beings. The divine–human relationship of love does depend on a beginning that is expressed, as usual, though a dialogue —not necessarily linked to words— and is destined by nature to last forever. This *perennial* character, though, is not currently assured, in the sense that there is a possibility of losing it as long as man's pilgrim condition lasts.

It should be noted, however, that what we say here has nothing to do with love understood simply as a sexual relationship which, even when it is legitimate, *is not an indispensable ingredient of the relationship of love*; and which becomes more poignant when it is not lawful and more deplorable when it develops aberrant characteristics. We must remember that sin *is the thing most opposite to a love* with which a sinful man has no association, once he has placed himself at the most opposite pole imaginable regarding any possible relationship of love: *He that committeth sin is of the devil: for the devil sinneth from the beginning. For this purpose the Son of God appeared,*

---

[2]Ps 2:7.

that he might destroy the works of the devil.[3] According to Jesus Christ, *everyone who commits sin is the slave of sin*;[4] thus he cannot ever be considered an enamored man, for love is essentially freedom (2 Cor 3:17).

The true loving relationship necessarily implies dialogue, expressed normally (but not exclusively) through words, as a necessary means to communicate and exchange feelings between lovers. In Infinite Love this dialogue takes place through the eternal *now* of only one Word, as Saint John of the Cross said. In created love, this relationship may exist before words do, *but never before dialogue.* For one simple look, otherwise silent, can contain a whole universe of communication and expression of feelings directed at the person who has caused it; so that a mysterious and ineffable dialogue has already been established between the love that has been offered and the love that answers; a dialogue that is quite capable of giving rise to the most binding and affectionate relationship of all the imaginable relationships between rational beings.

It should also be kept in mind that any form of love present in the creature, whether it be merely human or divine–human, is an analogy of the relations existing in the

---

[3] 1 Jn 3:8.

[4] Jn 8:34.

Bosom of the Trinity. Hence there is a necessary reference to the Divine Trinity —leaving aside the dissimilarities and paying attention to the similarities— in all forms of real human love; which is a further proof that man was created in the image of God.

In one way or another, as we have said above, the most ordinary form of loving dialogue takes place through words which produce such a degree of joy in the person who utters them and in him to whom they are addressed that it is beyond all possibility of description. The Bridegroom of the *Song of Songs*, for example, expresses his elation at hearing the voice of the Bride and his uncontrollable desire to hear it again:

> *O my dove,*
> *That art in the clefts of the rock,*
> *In the hollow places of the wall,*
> *Show me thy face,*
> *Let thy voice sound in my ears;*
> *For thy voice is sweet,*
> *And thy face comely.*[5]

The bride, on her part, is no less eager to hear the voice of the Bridegroom, without which (as it happens in

---

[5]Sg 2:14.

the most perfect form of human love, the divine–human love) she cannot live. Now the true disciple of Jesus Christ, who has heard quite well His offer of love, to which he, in turn, has given an affirmative answer, is in a position to understand that prayer is much more than mere dialogue, more than a simple means of petition or thanksgiving. And as God longs to hear the voice of the creature, the latter, in turn, whether he is aware of it or not, is starving and in desperate need of listening to God's voice. So the verse says:

> *In your orchard a small bird,*
> *In grief at your absence, sang with a sad sound;*
> *And, when your soft voice she heard,*
> *Quickly rose up from the ground,*
> *To search in her swift flight where you could be found.*[6]

We should stress that the greatest expressions and most perfect forms of love relationships in man are exclusively found in divine–human love —in its highest degrees— and not in merely human love, though it be legitimate or sanctified by grace. To which it should be added that,

---

[6] *CFC*, n. 9. In the Spanish original: *De tu vergel un ave/ por tu ausencia cantaba en desconsuelo;/ y oyó tu voz suave/ y, alzándose del suelo,/ a buscarte emprendió veloz su vuelo.*

because the divine–human love relationship is but a transcript of the perfect and mysterious communication expressed in the intimate dialogue of the loving *thou-I*, it is easier to understand that this relationship is between two persons and remains *closed* to all others: *To him that overcometh I will give to eat of the hidden manna, and will give him a white stone, and in the stone a new name written, which no man knoweth saving he that receiveth it.*[7] And hence the words exchanged between God and His creature are unintelligible to others and impossible to explain to those to whom they are not addressed; as the verse at the begining of this chapter suggests:

> *...Everything I told you and which you now know.*

Saint John of the Cross beautifully referred to this in his unsurpassed *Spiritual Canticle*:

> *All those that haunt the spot*
> *Recount your charm, and wound me worst of all*
> *Babbling I know not what*
> *Strange rapture, they recall,*
> *Which leaves me stretched and dying where I fall.*

---

[7]Rev 2:17.

XXV

Henceforth I call you not servants;
for the servant knoweth not what his lord doeth;
but I have called you friends;
for all things that I have heard of my Father
I have made known unto you.[1]

Now that I am at such an advanced age so as to call myself, properly speaking, an *old man*... but not without arousing great displeasure in many of my friends who consider this word taboo and who speak, rather, of being a *senior citizen* (I have never quite understood the aversion people have to calling things by their true names), I have finally realized that my whole life has been spent in a continuous and longing search, without my being aware of it;

---

[1] Jn 15:15.

and, what is more important, without even knowing what I was looking for.

In effect, much time passed before I finally realized that in my searching I have behaved, once again, as most men usually do. Very few men dare to confess that their life has been a huge void that they have desperately tried to fill with something which they have never found. Such has been my case, despite the many voices which have tried to tell me that what man is always looking for is nothing other than Joy; they alleged many reasons, none of which managed to bring peace to my soul; for nobody was ever able to explain to me what Joy is, and I was not able to find It anywhere.

I was confused and surrounded by my worries; and there always was somebody who would lovingly advise me to just forget about the problem and devote myself to *living my life*, which was seemingly the only thing that really mattered. However, I could never understand what *to live my life* exactly meant; and besides, I always ended up perceiving that, despite what my advisors persistently proclaimed, they themselves continued to eagerly search in pursuit of Joy. Finally I came to the conclusion that there has never been a man in the entire History of mankind who has ever abandoned this search. On the other hand, it has always been difficult for me to dismiss the impression that everything seems to indicate that our generation has struck a comfortable agreement by which it has conceded to live immersed in voluntary ignorance and excessive lies regarding our self–knowledge.

And yet, I clearly understand this now: there is no better way to condemn oneself to never finding Joy than by *seeking It in earnest.* For Joy is not something that can be sought and attained by Itself alone; It is always the consequence and the effect of the only reality that can cause It. That is why I can now surely affirm that they only achieve It *who are able to completely forget about It and stop looking for It.* For, indeed, what is Joy and which entity does It possess in Itself and by Itself?

And the answer seems as simple as it is surprising: In Itself, Joy has no entity; maybe that is why It never appears alone. Everything seems to indicate that It is nothing more than the fruit yielded by the most mysterious and sublime Reality that exists in the Universe... which is none other than love. For it is love alone which is the only thing capable of giving Joy, as something that necessarily follows from love's nature, or of leading to Perfect Bliss if you prefer to call Joy by another name. For it is clear that the enamored soul does not seek the Joy that the beloved person brings about in her, but rather *the beloved one who causes that Joy.* And I now feel like exclaiming about love what the great Saint Augustine said regarding Beauty: *Late have I loved you, O Beauty ever ancient and ever new, late have I loved you!* For love is the only Reality that fills everything, even the human heart; the same that, according to Dante, also *moves the sun and other stars.*

Thus, the awful drama of our time. We have stopped believing in love and, consequently, we have emptied everything that exists of *all content and meaning.* Modern man has come to believe that he can explain himself and the world without recourse to God. And because his understanding is limited, as well as small and obtuse, the resulting vision is equally disastrous and ridiculous.

I must admit that now, in my old age, the world around me is less comprehensible to me than it was during my younger years. For that line of thinking has also entered the theology of the modern Church, which continually feels panic at the prospect of being left behind by the world, or of not being in tune with it. Hence my astonishment when I see that the Pastoral activity of the *New Pentecost* has narrowed the scope of its horizon and has become a dwarfed and teratological theology. In this theology, God has been reduced to a purely human size, according to a *rational* understanding that is not willing to accept anything that exceeds it; consequently, it cannot possibly admit that God, out of pure love, *wanted to converse with man and to make him His friend.* How could the modern *critical and scientific exegesis* possibly concede that some particular expressions of the *Song of Songs* are more than just epithalamic or metaphorical language which excludes all intimacy and closeness between Divine Love and His creature? Thus, for example, the bride says:

> *Let him kiss me with the kisses of his mouth:*
> *For thy love is better than wine.*[2]

Or:

> *Come, my dove...*
> *Let me see thy face, let thy voice sound in my ears...*[3]

Which is an exclamation of love the Bridegroom addresses to the bride.

However, how can he believe such things who is not willing to acknowledge those realities which only love can bring about? Similarly, he who is not able to believe in

---

[2] Sg 1:2.
[3] Sg 2:14.

sacrifice or in self–denial or self–immolation out of love cannot possibly admit that someone has been able to give up his own life out of love for him. Hence the need felt by the *New Pastoral* activity for placing the dogma, and consequently worship, in such a narrow and *reasonable* condition so as to be understood by modern man. And so, is it strange that this new way of thinking held by modern Catholicism has reduced the Mass from being a Holy Sacrifice expressing Death out of love to the abject level of a pure and simple *meal of solidarity and brotherhood*? It is therefore sad to concede that not a few Catholics have now placed themselves at a level so menial as to be accepted and acknowledged by the modern world; *even though, in exchange, they have had to give up being recognized and accepted by God.*

More yet. Within the scope of the perfect and true love about which we are speaking (divine–human love — without thereby excluding true purely human love, which is an analogate), the lover knows, because this love is in its first phase of existence and therefore not yet a perfected and consummated love, that he cannot achieve love except through suffering; thus he would willingly accept suffering rather than Joy. For the only thing that matters to him is finding any way that leads faster and more safely to the beloved: Joy, suffering...? Who cares, if the whole point is to be with the beloved? So, let pain be welcome if it is indeed the best course, even to its consummation in death. For love always looks for totality; therefore, there is no other way to die that makes more sense than death caused by love:

> *His eyes fixed on my eyes; his gaze pierced me through*
> *Before Dawn awoke and made the sky rosy,*
> *And I was wounded so deeply that I knew*
> *If he took his soft gaze from me, then surely*
> *My life into sure death would turn so quickly.*[4]

The Doctrine of the Church has always maintained that Joy is man's last End —the *Beatitudo*, of which theologians have always spoken—, which is achieved through the *satiating contemplation of Truth*; and this is undoubtedly true.

But perhaps it may also be said that the *Beatitudo*, rather than the last end is *actually the penultimate*; for this Perfect Joy becomes real for the blessed only through the Possession of God. But if the notion about love which

---

[4] *CFC*, n. 32. In the Spanish original: *Sus ojos en los míos se posaron/ antes de que la aurora despertara,/ y de amor tan herido me dejaron/ que, si acaso de mí los apartara,/ mi vida en muerte pronto se trocara.*

we have outlined here is true and makes sense, it would validate the conclusion that a God merely contemplated (first step), but not yet possessed (second step), could not be the cause of perfect *Beatitudo*.

XXVI

Dialogue of love and silence.

Since dialogue is an essential part of any relationship of love, it is easy to see that each of the two lovers yearns to hear the voice of the other. It is irrelevant to resolve which of the two voices is more important since both are equally necessary for the existence of this relationship and because the sound of either voice coming from one of the lovers is a source of joy to the other: *Again there shall be heard in the cities of Judah, and in the streets of Jerusalem, the voice of joy, and the voice of gladness, the voice of the bridegroom, and the voice of the bride.*[1]

---

[1] Jer 33: 10–11.

God, on His part, eagerly wants to hear the voice of His creature, as He expresses through the mouth of the Bridegroom in the *Song of Songs*:

> *O my dove,*
> *That art in the clefts of the rock,*
> *In the hollow places of the wall,*
> *Show me thy face,*
> *Let thy voice sound in my ears;*
> *For thy voice is sweet,*
> *And thy face comely.*[2]

And the bride, as it could not be otherwise, also is troubled with excitement upon hearing the voice of the Bridegroom. For if any dialogue is necessarily a relationship between two, it should not be forgotten that everything in love is also reciprocal and bilateral:

> *The voice of my beloved!*
> *Behold, he cometh*
> *Leaping upon the mountains,*
> *Skipping over the hills.*[3]

---

[2] Sg 2:14.
[3] Sg 2:8.

Thus it is clear, once more, that a Plan of Salvation allegedly established by God unilaterally with respect to His creatures, without any need for acceptance or response from them (*anonymous Christianity*) would be completely meaningless. The relationship of intimate friendship that God has so ardently desired to establish with man would be destroyed and devoid of meaning: *Henceforth I call you not servants; for the servant knoweth not what his lord doeth. But I have called you friends.*[4] Consequently, the whole nature of the relationship of love would be reduced to nothing; with the necessary conclusion that any type of bond that God wishes to establish with man *would be anything but a loving relationship.* Friendship requires, by definition and of necessity, a free and voluntary consent, embodied in mutual affection, by the *two* friends.

The dialogue in the divine–human relationship of love establishes an intense communication between God and His creature, to the exclusion of everything else and with such a degree of privacy that is able to silence all other sounds that could hinder or distract this dialogue. This is a theme with which mystic poetry deals abundantly, stressing constantly the search for solitude, remote places, and silence, in addition to the total oblivion of anything

---

[4]Jn 15:15.

not in accord with the relationship of love; as this verse tries to show:

> *Following shepherds and sheep,*
> *I came to where the Loved One awaited me*
> *Hidden in hillsides so deep;*
> *And while I sought him softly*
> *Whistling noises from the jungle ceased to be.*[5]

Those who have not been able to silence the noise of the things around them think that God is a mute Being Who never communicates in intimacy with men. Love being the most exclusive Reality there is, It naturally requires detachment and oblivion of everything else: *Every one of you that doth not renounce all that he possesseth cannot be my disciple.*[6] And that is why the dialogue of divine–human love is always *silent* and takes place in solitude, quite apart from everything else:

---

[5] *CFC*, n. 6. In the Spanish original: *Siguiendo a los pastores/ busqué donde el Amado me esperaba/ oculto en los alcores./ Y al tiempo que me hablaba/ el susurro del viento se escuchaba.*

[6] Lk 14:33.

There, at my Beloved's side,
In the silence of Love's mutual sweet word,
I wished always to abide,
And in my ear he whispered
That he too, wounded by my love, has suffered.[7]

This explains the fact that this dialogue is accessible only to those who know how to love. For loving partially, with conditions or any kind of obstacles or circumstances in which anything is selfishly held back by the presumed lover makes love absolutely impossible. Too easily have Christians forgotten the commandment *thou shall love with thy whole heart and with thy whole soul and with thy whole mind.*[8] Which almost sounds like a tautology: is it possible to love in any other way? And while creatures are willing at any time to give their assent to any pseudo-love —which would only be an imitation of love—, God, Who is Truth and Infinite Love, would never accept that.

---

[7] *CFC.*, n. 59. In the Spanish original: *Acércate a mi lado/ mientras el cierzo sopla en el ejido,/ y deja ya el ganado,/ y cuéntame al oído/ si acaso por mi amor estás herido.*

[8] Mt 22:37.

Reality shows, however, that things so continually and strongly exert their demands on man that he ends up being attracted and enticed by them. God, in His Infinite goodness, has not failed to take this into consideration; therefore, He has moderated the attractiveness of all creation to a degree that is compatible with human capabilities. Hence His willingness to impose some silence, when circumstances demand it, on things, as stated in the *Song of Song*:

> *I adjure you, O daughters of Jerusalem,*
> *By the roes and the harts of the fields,*
> *That you stir not up, nor awake my beloved*
> *Till she please.*[9]

Despite this, we need to take into account —it must be said once more— the cooperation and consent of the human creature as required by the nature of things, without which the relationship of love would be impossible. For both the offering and the acceptance of love must be pronounced freely. That is why the Bridegroom, in His concern and care for the bride, adds *till she please* in the Poem's final petition.

---

[9]Sg 3:5.

This stanza clearly shows again that *anonymous Christianity* must be ruled out. This expression, in and of itself, implies a manipulation of the reality of love because love never allows anonymities but only intimate names, for it is a person–to–person relationship: *I have called thee by thy name.*[10] No wonder Jesus Christ makes the name precede the question addressed to Saint Peter about whether he loved Him more than the others: *Simon, son of John, lovest thou me more than these?*[11]

One of the most absurd monstrosities that the Father of Lies has ever invented is to introduce the notion of *anonymity* into the concept of love —which is always a person–to–person relationship, in complete freedom, in the most intimate and mutual understanding, and where the dearest *equal footing of the I and the thou* occurs. That is why Jesus Christ banished forever from love the *lord–servant* relation, replacing it with a relationship between *friends* (Jn 15:15). The dialogue of love requires from two lovers a mutual self–surrender and a self–giving in such total intimacy that it renders the *anonymity* implied by any lack of personal knowledge absolutely unthinkable:

---

[10] Is 45:3.

[11] Jn 21:15.

Come to me; be with me; stay.
While brisk North winds gust over the high meadow;
Leave the flock to find its way,
Whisper to me, faint and low,
That you feel wounded by my love's tender blow.[12]

---

[12] *CFC.*, n. 55. In the Spanish original: *Allí, junto al Amado/ mientras soplaba el cierzo en el ejido,/ a fuer de enamorado/ me susurró al oído/ que también por mi amor estaba herido.*

XXVII

My Bridegroom's voice is for me,
Like the wake of a ship deeply furrowing
Like winds that stir so lightly
Like a gentle whispering
Like the solemn moves of a night bird on wing.[1]

The bride of the *Song of Songs* exclaims with great eagerness upon hearing the voice of the Bridegroom:

The voice of my beloved! Behold, he cometh
Leaping upon the mountains,
Skipping upon the hills
My beloved is like a roe or a young hart.

---

[1] *CFC.* n. 75. In the Spanish original: *Es la voz del Esposo/ como la huidiza estela de una nave,/ como aire rumoroso,/ como susurro suave,/ como el vuelo nocturno de algún ave.*

> *He standeth behind our wall*
> *He looketh forth at the windows*
> *He peers through the lattice.*
> *My beloved spoke, and said unto me...*[2]

What more can an enamored bride wish than to hear the voice of the Bridegroom? *The words that I have spoken unto you, they are spirit, and they are life...*[3] *If you abide in me, and my words abide in you, you shall ask what you will, and it shall be done unto you.*[4] This voice is her reason for living; hence she ardently longs to listen to it at all times: at night or during the day, while she is awake, or during her sleep:

> *I sleep, but my heart waketh*
> *It is the voice of my beloved that knocketh.*[5]

In reality, nothing can be more ardently desired by an enamored soul than hearing the voice of God; before which all sufferings gain a new meaning, and the trials and hardships of this life vanish like smoke:

---

[2]Sg 2: 8–10.

[3]Jn 6:63.

[4]Jn 15:7.

[5]Sg 5:2.

> *In your orchard a small bird*
> *In grief at your absence, sang with a sad sound;*
> *And, when your soft voice she heard,*
> *Quickly rose up from the ground,*
> *To search in her swift flight where you could be found.*[6]

And since in love, as we have said many times, everything is bilateral and reciprocal, the Bridegroom of the *Song of Songs* desires nothing other than to hear the voice of the bride:

> *O my dove,*
> *That art in the clefts of the rock,*
> *In the hollow places of the wall,*
> *Show me thy face,*
> *Let thy voice sound in my ears;*
> *For thy voice is sweet,*
> *And thy face comely.*[7]

The words of Jesus Christ, as we have seen above, are indeed spirit and life for men; but most of the men to whom those words were addressed have inexplicably opted

---

[6] *CFC.* n. 9. In the Spanish original: *De tu vergel un ave/ por tu ausencia cantaba en desconsuelo;/ y oyó tu voz suave,/ y, alzándose del suelo,/ a buscarte emprendió veloz su vuelo.*

[7] Sg 2:14.

for hardening their hearts and ignoring them. The Letter to the Hebrews points at this fact: *Wherefore, as the Holy Spirit saith: Today if you will hear his voice, harden not your hearts, as in the rebellion.*[8] Jesus Christ Himself complained bitterly about the attitude of men: *If I say the truth, why do you not believe me?* And He added a clarification explaining that conduct: *He that is of God heareth the words of God; you therefore hear them not, because you are not of God.*[9]

It is for this reason that at this time of deep crisis that has befallen the Church —the most serious she has ever suffered throughout History— the words of the Gospel of Saint John have become most relevant: *He came unto his own, but his own received him not.*[10] Actually this same crisis has dictated that, at the present time, hardly anywhere in the world have Christians the opportunity to hear the Word of God. *For never before has the Christian world, and especially Catholics, been so deprived of the Word of God.* A statement that, harsh as it may seem, *applies to any level of Pastoral activity within the Church.* Saint Paul's words —quoting the Prophet Isaiah—, spoken in connection with a situation less severe than the current

---

[8] Heb 3: 7–8.

[9] Jn 8: 46–47.

[10] Jn 1:11.

one, seem to have been uttered for the present time: *But they have not all obeyed the gospel. For Isaiah saith, Lord, who hath believed what they have heard from us?*[11]

As is always the case, some might think that this statement is nothing but a personal opinion, far–fetched, and, of course, out of place. For never before has there been so much preaching or such prolific pastoral activity, which have been facilitated by modern mass media: sermons, speeches, statements, documents, books, and workshops given by Bishops and renowned theologians... all of it carried out in an environment filled with apparent *piety* where even the laity (men and women), not to mention nuns, have become preachers.

Which is very true. But the problem arises, and becomes even serious, when one looks into the *doctrinal* content of these preachings. Not only do they not speak about anything substantial —at best—, they also almost always validate the words of the Apostle Saint John: *They are of the world; therefore they speak of the world, and the world heareth them.*[12]

On the other hand, it is worthy to note that there now exists in the Church, as in the early days of her His-

---

[11]Rom 10:16.

[12]1 Jn 4:5.

tory, a boom of movements that appear to be in close proximity to the Holy Spirit and in deep affinity with His charisms —Pentecostal, Charismatic, Catechumenal, etc. A phenomenon that envisions the rebirth of a powerful new spirituality whose source is none other than the Spirit.

All this is also true. However, if we give a calm and in–depth analysis to this problem, then the following question does not seem to be unreasonable: to date, what *secure guarantees* have the Christian people that such impulses and inspirations really do come from the Holy Spirit?

XXVIII

The Great Unknown.

Within the *New Religion* observed by the post–conciliar Pastoral activity and which aims at carrying out a *New Evangelization*, there are various *Movements* (usually known by the generic name of *charismatic*) that possess —they claim— a multitude of gifts profusely received from the hands of the Spirit and which they are able to manage at will. This is not unusual, considering that, according to the teachings of Pope John Paul II, the Church has been favored, at the outset of the third millennium, with a *New Pentecost* that has flooded her with a shower of gifts.

We will leave aside for now the concern of some people at the onset of so many *Novelties* in a Church that, para-doxically, has always considered Herself traditional and immutable from the time Revelation was officially closed with the death of the last Apostle.

Charismatic Movements, in general, flaunt a way of relating to the Spirit which suggests that He is ready to endorse anyone who calls upon Him and will give him whatever He is asked with a promptness which brings to mind the automatic response of any vending–machine which operates at the punching of some buttons under the familiar command of *help yourself.*

However, it is difficult to accept that this way of imagining the Spirit and His *modus operandi* has anything to do with reality. Sound Doctrine has always considered the Spirit to be the most intimate reality, the very *heart* of God. He is unknown, infinitely delicate and subtle, mysterious and elusive, the One to Whom the *Love* of God is *attributed.* He is also Sovereign and Infinite Freedom —*Where the Spirit of the Lord is, there is liberty.*[1] As for His voice..., not even regarding it as an elusive whisper, wonderful and impressive, capable of leading to Perfect Joy and the Complete Truth would be tantamount to saying something accurate enough to even minimally express what it really is.

---

[1] 2 Cor 3:17.

According to Jesus Christ, *the Spirit bloweth where he will, and thou hearest his voice; but thou knowest not whence he cometh, and whither he goeth.*[2] But if love is already an inexplicable Mystery, what could one say about Him Who is the *Heart* of Infinite Love? Did the Fathers of the Church not have a great intuition when they called Him *The Great Unknown*? On the other hand, Love being supremely free in nature, how can anyone think that he has Him at his disposal Who is the very Voice of God speaking to whom He wants and whenever He wants; and about Whom it can never be known *whence he cometh, and whither he goeth*? For if man, during his earthly existence, can never understand how far love can go, *how could he grasp divine Love about Whom you never know where He comes from or whither He can go?*

Men have clearly heard Jesus Christ, Who is the Word of the Father. The Spirit, it is true, is the *Voice of God* and can be heard (nevertheless, hearing is not the same as listening or understanding); but only those who are immersed in Love and Truth can understand Him: *The Spirit of Truth, whom the world cannot receive, because it seeth him not, neither knoweth him; but you know him; for he dwelleth with you, and is in you*, said Jesus Christ

---

[2] Jn 3:8.

to His Apostles on the Night of His Farewell.[3] Only the Church, when she exercises her teaching office with the required conditions of infallible Magisterium, can impose the truth, since she speaks following the inspirations of the Holy Spirit.

Apart from this exceptional instance, whoever claims that he can listen at will to the Voice of Him Who is Love Himself (as though one can hear the words of a mechanical device by simply inserting a few coins) or dispose of His gifts, that person has no idea of what Love is: *the friend of the Bridegroom, who standeth and heareth him, rejoices greatly because of the Bridegroom's voice*, said John the Baptist.[4] But he was the *friend of the Bridegroom* and also *accompanied Him and was with Him*. But, except the Precursor himself, who would dare to presume that he is the friend of the Bridegroom and follows Him faithfully?

According to this, who can hear His voice...? As we have seen before and according to the Spirit Himself, only those who stay at His side and in whom He dwells (Jn 14:17); or, to put it briefly, those and only those hear His voice who are truly in love with God.

---

[3] Jn 14:17.

[4] Jn 3:29.

Hearing the Voice of God, as well as understanding and possessing true Love, is not something akin to picking apples whenever someone wills it; as we have said, it is something banned to the World. The bride herself in the *Song of Songs*, for example, admits her anguish caused by her difficulties in finding the beloved of her soul, while she longs to be able to do so:

> *Tell me, O thou whom my soul loveth,*
> *Where thou feedest, where thou makest thy flock*
>   *to rest at noon;*
> *That I may no more wander like a vagabond*
> *Beside the flock of thy companions.*[5]

Man could get a *possible* belief that he has listened to the Voice of the Spirit, but only though an indirect way and by studying *a posteriori* the fruits obtained. Not everyone who says that he follows His impulses can boast of being right. After reviewing the results, for example, both during the event and after the Second Vatican Council, it is difficult to give credence to the words of Pope John XXIII when he claimed that his calling of the Council was inspired by the Holy Spirit.

---

[5]Sg 1:7.

The truth is that the world is absolutely incapable of understanding true Love. Those who remain on the fringe of merely human love, and much more so those who mistake it for merely sexual activity, are far from understanding the significance of that mysterious and insinuating *whisper* which, without using words, speaks and says more than all the sounds and languages of the world; arousing sentiments which are ineffable and unimaginable to the human heart, were it not helped from on High. He communicates through a form of expression that only people truly in love can understand... and which, of course, is never able to depict all the infinite possibilities either of merely human love —no matter how pure it may be— or of that great gift which divine–human love is:

> *The calm, resplendent deep sea*
> *With peaceful, blue–white waves, rocked and gently stirred*
> *The soft echoes on the breeze,*
> *Songs of mermaids without word*
> *A sweet whisper of love that is barely heard.*[6]

---

[6] *CFC*, n. 44. In the Spanish original: *Los mares sosegados/ en ondas azuladas y serenas,/ los ecos apagados/ de cantos de sirenas/ un susurro de amor que se oye apenas.*

RECAPITULATION

And considered his work finished at the days end.
Although still bidding and barely commenced.
The bard sighed in his sorrow and fell silent:
Who would dare to sing to Beauty his lament.
And finally, with hurried pace he left then
His quill he left behind, it was forgotten.[1]

Rarely does a work of art satisfy its creator. Michelangelo, for example, felt that his *Moses* still lacked speech. Any work of art must necessarily be *finished*; but it is unlikely that the artist will consider the result to be a *faithful* transcript of what he had in his mind.

---

[1] *CFC,* n. 124: In the Spanish original: *Y dando la labor por acabada/ aun ni siquiera en ciernes comenzada,/ el bardo enmudeció con gran tristeza:/ ¿Quién osará cantar a la Belleza...?/ Y fuese al fin, en marcha apresurada,/ dejando atrás su péñola olvidada.*

This is even truer when it comes to human life. Very few men have been able to say, at the end of their existence, that they have lived a truly full life. Jesus Christ is the one Man Who could say with greatest truth, while dying on the cross and before breathing His last, *It is consummated.*[2] And Saint Paul, in turn, referring to the end of his earthly journey, ventured to say *I have fought a good fight, I have finished my course, I have kept the faith.*[3]

Be that as it may, the end of his life marks, for the average man, a time of acute depression brought about by the conviction that the work he was supposed to have done *was barely started* —and that in even the best of cases. Whatever was achieved, if anything, falls woefully short of the fulfillment of the task which was entrusted to him at the beginning of his existence; for the summit that was to be conquered was hardly glimpsed; it remained covered with perpetual snow and crowned with dense clouds that barely allowed a distant glance.

Nevertheless, there is no room for despondency; God has taken our limitations into account: *Fear not, little flock; for it hath pleased your Father to give you the kingdom.*[4] All one has to do is *to acknowledge* humbly that

---

[2]Jn 19:30.

[3]2 Tim 4:7.

[4]Lk 12:32.

everything is grace, as Bernanos said,[5] and fully accept the words of Jesus Christ: *Without me you can do nothing.*[6]

Moreover, it is normal that God sets for man goals which are seemingly impossible to achieve, given his status as a creature; as can be seen, for example, in the consummate command of Jesus: *Be you therefore perfect, as also your heavenly Father is perfect.*[7] Nevertheless, those goals are guiding lights that brighten the path of man's existence. It seems that a destiny which has been offered to man, and whose end reward is Eternal Life, is far more desirable when that end seems unreachable and that destiny hard, rather than when everything looks to be easily within reach and, therefore, not appropriate for those who are called to share the boundless glory of divine life.

But once the smallness of human achievements has been made manifest, God reveals His own approach: *Well done, good and faithful servant, because thou hast been faithful over a few things...*;[8] the Lord recognizes that the servant has been *faithful over a few things*, but this is not an obstacle to calling him *good and faithful* and assuring

---

[5]Georges Bernanos, *Diary of a County Priest*, Epilogue, *in fine*.

[6]Jn 15:5.

[7]Mt 5:48.

[8]Mt 25: 21.23; Lk 19:17.

him of his reward: *I will place thee over many things: enter thou into the joy of thy lord.*

Two things are clear in this passage, which should be read attentively, as any other passage of Holy Scripture should be read if we want to understand it and draw the appropriate conclusions.

First, the insignificance of human work is made clear, whatever the task yet to be achieved or already completed may be; which is normal if we consider that the goal is set in the infinite: *Be ye therefore perfect, as also your heavenly father is perfect.* Indeed, human smallness would fill anyone with dismay whose thinking is free from prejudice; as is written in the *Book of Job: What is man that thou shouldest magnify him? and that thou shouldest set thine heart upon him?*;[9] or as the Psalms also corroborate: *What is man, that thou art mindful of him? or the son of man, that thou visitest him?*[10] In reality there are always reasons to think that anything man does, no matter how transcendent it may seem and regardless of his righteousness (which is presumed at all times), in truth, he has been *faithful in a few things* only. It is not surprising then that there may be times when man, overwhelmed by

---

[9] Job 7:17.
[10] Ps 8:5.

the feeling of his own Nothingness, becomes so anxious as to believe that he will not be able to find God anywhere:

> *To the distant stars I climbed*
> *For small vestige of your footprints to find.*
> *Hoping some to sight,*
> *While walking toward the Sun, from the Moon at night.*[11]

We must stress the fact that the man referred to here is a *good and faithful servant*, as the passage expressly states. Therefore, any ill will or rejection of the loving offer made by God are to be ruled out.

Nevertheless, despite the good will of the creature, his contribution is insignificant: *because thou hast been faithful over a few things...* And yet it will provide the basis upon which the grandeur of the established relationship is founded; as we shall soon see.

This said, we can easily appreciate that the corollary of the passage is very consoling. It makes apparent again the enormous distance between what is grandiose and what is miniscule, finite and infinite, the possibilities of man and the magnificence of a God Who overcomes an infinite

---

[11] *CFC*, n. 7. In the Spanish original: *Subí hasta las estrellas/ en busca de vestigios de tus huellas,/ por si encontraba alguna/ caminando hacia el Sol, desde la Luna.*

distance... to show His total Love for His creature and to be requited in the same way.

The smallness of His creature has not been an obstacle for God to pour out the strength of His Love and the largesse of His generosity: *I will place thee over many things: enter thou into the joy of thy lord.* Once more *power is made perfect in infirmity*;[12] divine magnificence and grandeur overcome human insignificance and smallness. The Book of Psalms, for example, as we have seen, after affirming that the human creature does not deserve much attention from God, adds:

> *Thou hast made him a little less than the angels,*
> *Thou hast crowned him with glory and honour:*
> *And hast set him over the works of thy hands.*
> *Thou hast subjected all things under his feet,*
> *All sheep and oxen:*
> *Moreover the beasts also of the fields.*
> *The birds of the air, and the fishes of the sea.*[13]

And since the divine–human love relationship is governed by the rules of reciprocity and bilateralism, as is every true love relationship, the condition of *equality*, also

---

[12] 2 Cor 12:9.

[13] Ps 8: 6–9.

a characteristic of every true loving relationship, becomes evident here through the aspect of *totality*; whereby both parties give each other all they are and all they have because they love each other in and with the same Love. At this point in the divine–human relationship, the human creature is *on a par* with his Lord, since both surrender to each other in complete *totality*: an infinite Love Who gives Himself *entirely* and a finite love that also surrenders himself *completely*.

This theory of perfect equality in the relationship of love, as required by the laws of perfect Love, is extensively discussed in detail in the doctrine of Saint John of the Cross:

> *The soul gives to the Beloved, Who is God Himself, what He had given to it. Herein it pays the whole debt, for the soul giveth as much voluntarily with inestimable joy and delight, giving the Holy Spirit as its own of its own free will, so that God may be loved as He deserves to be. Herein consists the inestimable joy of the soul, for it sees that it offers to God what becomes Him in His Infinite Being. Though it be true that the soul cannot give God to God anew, because He is always Himself in Himself, still it does so, perfectly and wisely, giving all that He has given it in requital of His love; this is to give as it is given, and God is repaid by this gift of the soul; nothing less could repay Him. He receives this gift of the soul as if it were its own, with kindness and grace, in the sense I have explained; and in that gift He loves it anew, and gives Himself freely to it, and the soul also loves Him anew. Thus, there is in fact a mutual interchange of love between the soul and*

God in the conformity of the union, and in the matrimonial surrender, wherein the goods of both, that is the divine essence, are possessed by both together, in the voluntary giving up of each to the other. God and the soul say, the one to the other, what the Son of God said to the Father in Saint John (17:10), "All My things are Thine, and Thine are Mine, and I am glorified in them."[14]

It is worth recalling two important and even essential points. First, we are in the realm of the mysterious reality that is Love; in which, once again, what a created mind could never have imagined does happen. Secondly, the issue we are talking about depends entirely on grace, without which nothing of what has been said here would enjoy any effectiveness.

God willed that the divine–human relationship of love should develop according to the rules of a true and perfect love relationship in which *everything* that belongs to one becomes the possession of the other in a perfect reciprocity which makes actual what the bride of the *Song of Songs* says: *My beloved is mine and I am his*;[15] which, in turn, is but an echo of the well–known saying of love, *everything I have is yours, and yours is mine* This creates a situation —made possible by Love alone— in which, while the personality of each party remains intact, everything that one

---

[14]Saint John of the Cross, *Living Flame of Love,* III, 79.

[15]Sg 2:16.

party *gives and receives* is reciprocally *received and given* by the other, thus eliminating any trace of inequality in this relationship: *Henceforth I call you not servants... but I have called you friends.*[16]

This doctrine was definitively established by Jesus Christ in His Farewell Speech at the Last Supper: [Father] *I have made known thy name to them, and will make it known; that the love, wherewith thou hast loved me, may be in them, and I in them.*[17] *And the glory which thou hast given me, I have given to them; that they may be one, as we also are one... I in them, and thou in me; that they may be made perfect in one.*[18] *That they all may be one, as thou, Father, in me, and I in thee; that they also may be one in us.*[19]

Thus the Love of God is poured out in man *by the Holy Ghost, who is given to us.*[20] And since He is the same Holy Spirit by which and in which man loves God, a perfect

---

[16] Jn 15:15.

[17] Jn 17:26.

[18] Jn 17: 22–23.

[19] Jn 17:21.

[20] Rom 5:5.

bond of love is established between them.[21] It follows that since God and man each gives his own self to the other in that union which the Holy Spirit has made possible —*that the love, wherewith thou* [Father] *hast loved me, may be in them, and I in them*—, a status of *equality* in Love is established between God and man: God loves man in the Holy Spirit, and man corresponds through the same Spirit; Who, in this way, is exhaled (*spiratio*) by both together, as Saint John of the Cross said in his prose commentaries to his poetry. The constant *actuality* of their mutual self-giving makes it possible for their relationship of love to remain unbroken in this mutual offering–reception which, in turn, as a feature of perfect Love, is intended to be enduring.

The infinite distance between the Eternal and what is temporary, between the Necessary and the contingent, between Highest Perfection and imperfection has been bridged, annihilated; now man is something more than just a friend to God, for he has been granted a participation in His Divine Nature (2 Pet 1:4).

As we have said, Saint John of the Cross speaks about a mutual *spiration* by God and man of the Holy Spirit

---

[21]The Fathers also considered the Holy Spirit as *nexus duorum* in the bosom of the Trinity. This term can be applied here provided that we take analogy into account.

and His presence in the soul; which is not surprising when one considers that love is always between two persons: God and man in this case. In this way, a reciprocal offer–reception on the part of two persons in love with each other is born; which, according to Saint John, brings about a veritable *transformation* of the soul in God, and even in the three Persons of the Holy Trinity:

> *This aspiration of the air is a certain faculty which the soul says that God will give her in the communication of the Holy Spirit, Who, like one breathing, raises the soul by His divine aspiration, informs her, strengthens her, so that she too may breathe in God with the same aspiration of love which the Father breathes in the Son, and the Son in the Father, which is the Holy Spirit Himself, Who is breathed into the soul in the Father and the Son in that transformation so as to unite her to Himself; for the transformation will not be true and perfect if the soul is not transformed in the Three Persons of the Most Holy Trinity in a clear and manifest degree. This aspiration of the Holy Spirit in the soul, whereby God transforms her in Himself, is to the soul a joy so deep, so exquisite, and so grand that no mortal tongue can describe it, no human understanding, as such, can conceive it in any degree; for even that which passes in the soul with respect to the communication which takes place in her transformation wrought in this life cannot be described, because the soul united with God and transformed in Him breathes in God that very divine aspiration which God breathes Himself in the soul when she is transformed in Him.*[22]

---

[22]Saint John of the Cross, *Spiritual Canticle*, Stanza XXXIX, 3.

Perhaps the expression *transformation* of the soul into God as used by Saint John is not exactly appropriate. It goes without saying that Saint John always clearly stresses, throughout his doctrine, the substantial and permanent distinction between God and the soul; therefore, it would be unfair and unreasonable to somehow claim that he subscribes to anything contrary. This is mainly a problem of language. The term *transformation* has an ambivalent meaning —simple *change of aspect* or a *substantial change*— which may not coincide with the one which our Saint meant in his sixteenth–century language; hence the danger of pantheism.

Leaving aside the fact that it is metaphysically impossible for one person to change into another, it must be said that, truly speaking, the creature that loves [the lover] would not want to *be transformed* into the beloved. Such a suggestion would be so absurd that merely advancing the possibility would be utterly rejected by the lover, consciously or unconsciously. In the relationship of love the other is loved as *other*, contemplated as *other*, desired as *other*. The *other* is someone attractive and charming as a person completely *distinct* from the lover; so much so that if the *other* ever ceases being the *other* the relationship of love would immediately disappear, because it is always based upon the opposition of *I–thou*. Moreover, giving and receiving would be impossible if there were no *one* and *another* as different and distinct beings. Hence the loving *I* always thinks of the beloved *thou* as someone opposed to himself with whom he can carry on a *dialogue* of love which, otherwise, would be a mere *monologue* leading to absurd narcissism.

Any notion, therefore, of one person being *transformed* into another or being *fused* with another into a third must be rejected. What then would be the exact significance of the mutual *identification* of the lovers, or the reciprocal possession of one by the other? What does the bride of the *Song of Songs* really mean when she says: *My beloved is mine, and I am his?*[23] Or what does Jesus Christ imply when He affirms that *He that eateth my flesh, and drinketh my blood, dwelleth in me, and I in him. As the living Father hath sent me, and I live by the Father; so he that eateth me, even he shall live by me?*[24]

Answering these questions would involve delving into the essence of the most profound Mystery of Love. Therefore, there is no approach other than approximations and the ruling out of possibilities, for this is a mystery more easily intuited than explained.

---

[23] Sg 2:16.
[24] Jn 6: 56–57.

To say, for example, as a possible answer, that these expressions are tantamount to an exchange of feelings, does not explain a reality which goes much further and is far more complex; nor can we answer by resorting to the notions of possession or power of disposing that each lover has over the other, for the problem would not be settled and this answer would raise new and more subtle questions. And so on.

Perhaps this passage of Saint Paul in his *Letter to the Galatians* (2:20) can be used as the starting point for our reflection and study: *I live; yet not I, but Christ liveth in me.*

The Apostle begins by saying that in his relationship with Christ he is and remains being himself and no other, thus asserting his personal and non–renounceable identity —*I live.* Then he says something that seems to be a contradiction —*yet not I.* In this second phrase, the adversative conjunction *yet* undoubtedly means an essential departure from the previous one in which Saint Paul stated the identity of his own self. But this variation cannot negate the first statement; otherwise the whole thing would be a meaningless contradiction. The logical bridge between these two proclamations and their answer is in the third phrase —*but Christ liveth in me.* The mystery remains, however, for we have not reached a fully satisfactory answer; after all, what does it mean that *Christ liveth in me*?

Perhaps we might as well accept the idea that Saint Paul was not more explicit because that is all he could say. All mysteries have a threshold beyond which no human being can go; nevertheless, they are significant inasmuch as they *induce* ideas that have a proper and sufficient function, as well as being necessary and indispensable, in this life, and which will lead us to total understanding in the other, *But when that which is perfect is come, then that which is in part shall be done away.*[25]

But then, is it still possible to maintain that the phrase *Christ liveth in me* has any meaning for human understanding? It must have some otherwise we would be implying that the Apostle spoke with the intention of saying nothing, just for the sake of speaking.

Perhaps it is possible to think, maintaining of course due respect to this mystery, that, while a fusion of persons can never be admitted, an identity of lives, or of wills if you want, can be otherwise confirmed. In this sense, Saint Paul would be stating that *the life of Christ is now his own life,* which he has freely exchanged for that of Christ's. Put another way, *he has made his the feelings, the thoughts, and*

---

[25] 1 Cor 13:10.

the will of Christ, which are now governing his existence. And Saint Paul does this without renouncing his own will and while maintaining the integrity of his own personality, because *what he wants now* is to do the will of Christ in everything; he does not wish anything otherwise. This does not mean that a merger of wills has occurred; such union would negate Saint Paul's personality, rendering the relationship of love impossible. There is rather an identification of wills by which the Apostle wanted *and still wants, now and at all times,* to do nothing but the will of Christ; one could even speak of a moment *constantly updated* in which *he wants and desires just what Christ wants and desires.* Now the circle of perfect Love is closed by reciprocity; for *Christ also wants and desires the same as His Apostle wants.* Saint Paul, therefore, far from abdicating or relinquishing his will and freedom, does the opposite: he wants and desires, with a powerful intensity and profound freedom, such as he has never wanted before.

Someone may object that this reasoning is apparently incompatible with the power of man to perform his own personal actions using his own will and freedom; will and freedom which have been allegedly surrendered completely to Christ and, therefore, they no longer belong to him nor can he freely dispose of them.

It should be noted, however, that such self–giving or donation takes place in an *actual moment* that occurs in a non–intermittent, never–interrupted *now*. Let us not forget that what makes a rational being a person is his power to relinquish everything... except this power itself. Otherwise, should he lose this power, his condition as a person would disappear. In this way, it is possible for the creature to offer his being —in an instant which is always current and therefore continuous— and yet remain himself. This allows the Apostle to say in the same phrase and without any contradiction, *I live; yet not I.*

A clearer approach to the problem could be as follows: Given that true love is *total* donation of the lover to the beloved, a serious objection may be raised: if the lover really gives *everything*, then he is deprived even of his power to give, which is the *essential element constituting* a person as such person; therefore, the lover would cease to be a person. If, however, he does not give *everything*, one could no longer speak of a *total* self–giving.

The solution is that the self–giving of one's personhood, far from being temporary, is an act that enjoys perfect and *perpetual actuality*: self–giving, indeed, is a real act and, therefore, takes place in absolute *totality*. But it is done, and continues to be done, in the perfect actuality of a perennial action which was done and is *still being done*. Hence the person certainly gives everything, but does not cease being a person; his self–giving is taking place in an enduring and perfect *now*, which makes it possible for him to keep what constitutes his personhood. That is why Saint Paul says in his First Letter to the Corinthians (13:8) that *charity never ends.*

Still, the following question could be posed: If the power to give and, therefore, the power to receive in perfect reciprocity are the elements that formally constitute a person, then what shall we say about the Holy Spirit within the Mystery of the Holy Trinity, Who is Perfect Love and the foundation, source, and analogical point of reference of all created love relationships? In what sense could those essential elements be an affirmation of the Holy Spirit as a Divine Person?

We know that act is the perfection of potency. Within the Trinity, potency and act are the same thing. Hence the Holy Spirit is, properly speaking, potency —of self–giving and receiving— in *perfect actuality.* So He can be said to be both *total donation and total reception.* This is why He is the Divine Person to Whom the name *Gift* can be attributed most properly, as the Fathers indicated. In effect, the Holy Spirit is total and complete *Gift* because He is *self–giving*, and total and complete *Gift* since He is *reception.* Therefore, to Him, better than to the Father or to the Son, the name *Love of God*, or also *Heart of God* corresponds.

And at this point *this work must come to an end.* In effect, our search is for Supreme Beauty; it must, therefore, stop at some point. Despite the fact that Supreme Beauty seems virtually unattainable —at least for now— and that She can only be glimpsed *from a distance and far away*, one can still find vestiges, fragments, and semblances of uncreated Beauty which, for the time being, suffice to feed hope in the hearts of those who seek Her integrally. Actually, it can be said that what has been gained *already* amply substantiates what has *not yet* been grasped.

Who will dare to sing to beauty? Only dreamers, of course. But saints and true poets are included in that category; hence, they save the world from what is prosaic and purely practical prose; that is, from a way of life which is unable to look upwards at all that is beyond the horizon.

Launch out into the deep![26] Those who do not dare to venture are the ones who remain on the shore... and are never able to attain anything. Whereas those who dare to set out in the risky and unpredictable pursuit of Beauty —that is, the pursuit of holiness— are the ones who accept the risk of ending in failure... And surely indeed that may be what happens. But would anyone dare to deny that in their attempt with the possibility of failure is where they will find victory? *Who would dare to sing to beauty* or, put another way, *who will attempt to reach the joy of contemplating infinite beauty*? Perhaps the daring act of faithfulness was enough of a response to the seemingly distant call of Love —or was it His voice whispering too closely into man's ear? Who knows? It was then, when man tried to respond generously to the offer made to him, that the smallness or nothingness of what he had

---

[26]Lk 5:4.

accomplished was, nevertheless, enough to manifest the greatness of his heart which, being too daring and trustful because it was excessively in love, may deserve, for that very reason, the joy of achieving the possession and intimacy of its Lord. *Well done, good and faithful servant; because thou hast been faithful over a few things, I will place thee over many things; enter thou into the joy of thy lord.*[27]

---

[27]Mt 25: 21.23; Lk 19:17.

Index of Quotations

from the

New Testament

29, **24, 28, 206**

6: 51, **98**

56, **114**

56–57, **98, 221**

63, **198**

8: 12, **21**

34, **177**

46–47, **200**

9: 4, **46, 61**

10: 3–4, **121**

4–5, **88**

10, **111**

16, **75**

11: 28, **121**

12: 31, **154**

13: 33, **61**

34–35, **27**

14: 4, **22**

6, **22, 142, 152**

17, **101, 206**

25–26, **84**

27, **152**

15: 5, **211**

7, **198**

15, **181, 191, 195, 217**

16: 5–7, **61**

7, **131**

11, **154**

22, **131, 152**

17: 10, **216**

11, **131**

15, **54**

21, **217**

22–23, **217**

26, **217**

19: 30, **210**

20: 13, **62**

21: 15, **115, 195**

HECHOS DE LOS APÓSTOLES

1: 11, **129**

20: 35, **41**

ROMANOS

2: 6, **54**

4: 18, **141, 159**

1 JUAN

APOCALIPSIS

INDEX

OF

SONGS

CONTENTS

Florilegium